A Flower Grows in Ireland

"When you come so close to death, you see how great life is. People tend to forget easily, but when you lose your legs, you have to live with it the rest of your life ...I can say with a true heart that I feel no bitterness toward the people who done it. The Lord has helped me a lot."

This is the real story of Northern Ireland's conflict—as the Irish themselves see it and say it. Jimmy Stewart, quoted above, is a machine shop worker who lost his legs in the bloody Abercorn disaster. He struggled with his fear and hatred, and a new understanding for those who maimed him was born.

Alec Gould, a Protestant, was mourning his son who had been murdered by Catholics, when drunken rioters threatened a Catholic neighbor's home. The rioters dispersed when they found Alec in front of his neighbor's door, warning them they would have to take him first.

Then there is the Rev. Sam Eliot,

(*Continued on back flap*)

A FLOWER GROWS IN IRELAND

A FLOWER GROWS IN IRELAND

RON WILSON

David C. Cook Publishing Co.
ELGIN, ILLINOIS—WESTON, ONTARIO

ACKNOWLEDGMENTS

Quote on page 63 reprinted from Christian Life
magazine, © 1974, Christian Life, Inc., Wheaton, Ill.
Quote by Father Jerome McCarthy reprinted with permission of Commonweal, © 1974.

A FLOWER GROWS IN IRELAND

Copyright © 1976 David C. Cook Publishing Co.

David C. Cook Publishing Co., Elgin, IL 60120

Printed in the United States of America

Library of Congress Catalog Number: 75-18646

ISBN: 0-912692-78-2

To my brothers and
sisters in Northern Ireland
who are joining hands and
hearts across the ancient barriers.

CONTENTS

PREFACE

I visited Northern Ireland for the first time in the fall of 1969 as a journalist. That was the year Ulster attracted international attention through television coverage of the riots and violence. The ugly sectarian sores which had scarred the province for centuries broke out once again on the peaceful veneer of Irish life.

I was appalled at what appeared to be a struggle right out of the seventeenth century, yet encouraged as I learned how God was working in the lives of many men and women in the midst of that outwardly hopeless situation.

In the years since, I have kept abreast of the situation, aware that much of the story was not being told. This is not a condemnation of the media. Generally speaking they accurately report and interpret the political events. What's happening on a deeper level, especially in the spiritual realm, goes untold.

I visited Northern Ireland again in the fall of 1974, and this book is a result of that trip. It is intended to give a feel of life in that unfortunate country, to let you meet the people I met, experience their life the way I did and gain enough insight into the background to dispel some of the myths which persist about Northern Ireland.

I have touched on politics only as I felt it was necessary to accomplish my purpose. Many other facets of life I have left untouched. For example, most books on Northern Ireland depart for at least one chapter to consider the Republic in the South. I feel it would take another book to do justice to that subject.

It is impossible to write about Northern Ireland without using the terms "Protestant" and "Catholic." But these terms today have more social and political connotations than they do religious or theological. They refer to two communities which happen to be in conflict, and the people who are called Protestant or Catholic often have no strong church allegiance. They are Protestant or Catholic because of their political and social positions. At the moment, however, there seems to be no better terms so I will use these. As the story unfolds I trust it will be clear how woefully inadequate and often misleading these terms are.

I am sure that the many friends I have in Northern Ireland, from both sides of the conflict, will be dismayed as they read parts of this book, and it will confirm their suspicions that an outsider can never understand. I only hope they will consider it all the more carefully because it does come from an outsider and that they will remain my friends.

I am especially thankful to many of these people for their openness and patience, for the extra mile which they often went to help me and for their willingness to spend hours in conversation. This is really their book.

The rhetoric and the writing about Northern Ireland would fill volumes. This sampler of quotes — like the book to follow — will begin to give the reader a feel for the complexity of the case. As a Belfast citizen said, in the most-quoted of quotes about Northern Ireland, "Anyone who isn't confused here really doesn't understand what's going on."

Northern Ireland is neither a nation nor a state. Legally it is a subordinate part of the United Kingdom. Historically, it is an insubordinate part. — RICHARD ROSE

Remove the British and raise the tricolor over Dublin Castle tomorrow and Ireland's problems will remain, because Ireland's problems are economic and social.
— JAMES CONNOLLY, 1897

The Charismatic Movement in Ireland is certainly the most powerful and surprising work of the Holy Spirit that I have seen in years. — DAVID DU PLESSIS

In Ireland there are two acceptable reactions to a crisis. The first is to get down on your knees and pray to God. The second is to go down on one knee, lift a gun and try to shoot the head off your opponent. — ROSITA SWEETMAN

The heart of the solution we offer today is the call for immediate withdrawal of British troops from Ulster and the establishment of a united Ireland.
— SEN. EDWARD M. KENNEDY

A healthy nation is as unconscious of its nationality as a healthy man is of his bones. But if you break a nation's nationality it will think of nothing else but getting it set again. It will listen to no reformer, to no philosopher and no preacher, until the demands of the Nationalists are granted. It will attend to no business, however vital, except the business of unification and liberation.
— BERNARD SHAW

God is giving us a vision of a land healed by His power and united in His love. The future is not with those who hate.
— CECIL KERR

> Ye Loyalists of Ireland
> Come, rally round the Throne!
> Thro' weal or woe prepare to go,
> Make England's cause your own;
> Remember your allegiance,
> Be this your Battle Cry,
> For Protestant Ascendancy
> In Church and State we'll Die!
> (POPULAR LOYALIST BALLAD)

Northern Ireland has too many Roman Catholics and twice as many Protestants, but very few Christians. — ANONYMOUS

The biggest repair job of all in Northern Ireland is going to be to the damaged minds of our young people.
— MONICA PATTERSON

No surrender
    — Protestant battle cry in 1689
    — Graffiti on walls in N. Ireland in 1976

If my people, which are called by my name, should humble themselves, and pray, and seek my face, and turn from their wicked ways; then will I hear from heaven, and will forgive their sin, and will heal their land.

— II CHRONICLES 7: 14

Disaster at the Abercorn

CHAPTER ONE

Disaster at the Abercorn

THE BLACK EXHAUST OF THE BUSES in the Royal Avenue and High Streets, and all through Belfast's busy shopping center, mixed with the moist air to choke the Saturday shoppers.

Jimmy Stewart had left the machine shop on the Shankill at noon and had taken the bus to the center to do a bit of shopping. It was a few weeks before Easter and the shops were jammed.

Janet Bereen, a radiographer at the Royal Victoria Hospital, mused on Paris in the spring as she pushed through the crowds. She had a ticket to fly there on holiday later that week. The McNern sisters, Rosaleen and Jennifer, shopped for an even happier occasion. Rosaleen was engaged to a man from Killybegs in County Donegal. The wedding wouldn't be until August but they were getting a start on Rosaleen's trousseau.

The "troubles," as they are called in Northern Ireland, had gone on for more than three years. Riots, bombings, thousands of families burned or chased from their homes, a lone pedestrian shot as he walked to work in the early dawn, political murder.

But, as the minister of commerce had said just the day before, "It's still business as usual in Ulster, despite the gunmen and the bombers." People adjusted. "Fiddler on the Roof" was in the third week at the Royal Avenue Theatre. The Ulster Bus Tours advertised a four-day package to Scotland for 27 pounds and a seven-day package to England and Wales for 46 pounds.

In Castle Lane in the heart of the shopping center, a throng of mostly women crowded the popular Abercorn Restaurant.

Janet Bereen had ducked in for tea. So had Rosaleen and Jennifer McNern. At 4 p.m. Jimmy Stewart glanced up and noticed the clock, then headed toward the Abercorn.

On the corners the news hawks began a brisk sale of the *Belfast Telegraph.* "Police Shoot a Bomber Dead," the paper headlined. Three men had tried to plant a bomb outside the Olympia Business Machines factory, but a police car approached before they could get away. The police killed one and wounded another, but a third one in the getaway car drove off. Other items in the news included a blind man who had learned to ski and was ready to try the Alps and a political item on a Roman Catholic as the Alliance party's new leader.

About 4:15 p.m. a man got up from a table in the middle of the Abercorn, moved over to the cashier, paid his bill and walked out. He left behind a small package. At 4:28 p.m., March 4, 1972, the Royal Ulster Constabulary Communications Center received a call from a General Post Office operator. An anonymous person had just telephoned to say there was a bomb in Castle Lane. The RUC immediately ordered police to the area but 60 seconds later the bomb exploded.

In the street outside the Abercorn, the blast blew shoppers from their feet and showered glass and debris over them. Inside it was panic. Smoke, screaming and yelling, tables on end, the ceiling coming down.

Jimmy Stewart had finished his coffee and had just stood to his feet when it happened. The next thing he knew he was on the floor, the sting of acrid smoke in his lungs and shock waves going through him.

Civic workers arrived within minutes and began laying out the injured in the street and treating them for cuts, bruises and shock. Both Rosaleen and Jennifer McNern were seriously hurt and were bundled into an ambulance.

As the injured began to arrive at the Royal Victoria Hospital, Janet Bereen's father, a doctor, took part in operations on the victims. He was unaware that his daughter had been killed in the same disaster. Both of the McNern girls had their legs amputated. Rosaleen lost an arm and an eye besides.

4

Jimmy Stewart couldn't figure out what was happening to him. He thought for a moment it was the end, then he managed to roll over on his back. But he couldn't sit up. He reached down and felt the blood oozing out of his legs, but he couldn't grasp what had happened. In moments he was in an ambulance on the way to the hospital and then he was in real agony.

He knew others who had been hurt through the troubles — one blinded by gunfire, another killed. He had lived most of his life in the Shankill, a tough, lower-class Protestant section close to the Ardoyne, an equally tough Catholic district. That put him right in the middle of the riots.

Mackies, the textile engineering firm where he worked, sat right on the border line of the Shankill and the Catholic Falls Road section. A year before the workers from Mackies' had come out for lunch one day to find the army face to face with Catholic crowds. The workers began to jeer at the crowds and pelt them with "Belfast confetti," a mixture of ball bearings and machine shop shavings.

Belfast had once been the center of the Irish linen trade and the Shankill was dotted with mills. When the mills were working the hardest in the late 1800's, a tireless young Christian worker named Amy Carmichael worked among the mill girls. One day she approached the owner of a mill on the Cambrai Street and asked for a slice of land on which to build a hall. Then she raised 500 pounds and built a structure to hold 500 people. It was called the Welcome Hall and stood around the corner from where Jimmy Stewart lived. Once it was just for the shawlies (what they called the mill girls because they wore shawls rather than "respectable" hats). But now it was a gospel hall for everyone, and Jimmy Stewart's mother had found Christ there some 30 years before.

The Welcome Hall was a landmark for Jimmy. He went there as a child. He walked past it day after day, month after month. Then one night he found himself in its back room on his knees. He had, in his own words, "been brought up in the way of the Gospel. I knew I had to be saved but wasn't willing to take the step toward Christ. Came a time when I was on the booze.

5

"God moved in my heart in September and I came under the conviction of sin. I didn't know what was happening. I started to ask my mother about such things as life and death . . . and that weekend I began to seek after God.

"September 29, 1968, a Sunday night, I found myself in the Welcome Hall after many years of being out of it. On that day I heard the Gospel, saw my need of a Savior and started to ask questions." Later that evening, on his knees in the back room beside the pastor, he asked Jesus Christ to come into his heart and be his Savior.

Jimmy Stewart's life changed then. He spent his spare time working with children, in special meetings and in Sunday school. He also met a young lady, Florrie Orr, at the Hall and began spending time with her.

Then came the Abercorn disaster. Before that Saturday was over, Jimmy Stewart's legs had been amputated.

"When they tell you you've lost two legs it's quite an ordeal . . . people try to give you comfort . . . who can you turn to . . . ? I saw myself as a helpless cripple and asked for grace to bear the burden . . . and He gave it to me."

Florrie Orr came to see Jimmy in the hospital. Night after night for ten months she came. And when he left the hospital for the rehabilitation center, she came to visit him there. A year later, with artificial legs and canes, Jimmy Stewart slowly walked down the aisle of the Welcome Hall with Florrie, his bride.

The story made the front page of the *Belfast Telegraph* and quoted Florrie as saying, "The explosion came as a real blow to me. I am a Christian and I believe the Lord wanted us to be together. I always knew we were right for each other.

"You just had to admire Jimmy's fight for recovery. It was a long hard struggle and his spirit was amazing. People used to dread visiting him in the beginning because they didn't know what to say. But it always ended up with them going away cheered up."

Jimmy Stewart has told his story many times. And in his sing-song Belfast accent adds, "I can say with a true heart that I feel no bitterness toward the people who done it. I feel it has given me great insight into life . . . when you come so close to death you see how great life is . . . people tend to forget easily, but when you lose your legs, you have to live with it the rest of your life . . . I think I've overcome it pretty well. The Lord has helped me a lot."

Right after the accident the *Belfast Telegraph* described him as "brave Jimmy Stewart." Then they featured Jimmy again when he got married. But outside of Northern Ireland few people have heard of him.

The story of Christians struggling with fear and faith in Northern Ireland hasn't gained much attention in the press. How is God working there? What are Christian people doing? Are believers really throwing rocks? And is it, when you get right down to it, a religious conflict?" Few publications have tackled these questions. Few have looked in depth at the evangelical community. Few have sought out the Jimmy Stewarts or tried to find the Christian life and witness that is there.

Of course it's a little harder in Northern Ireland to separate true Christianity from churchiness. Religion obviously means more to people in Northern Ireland than in most countries. In the 1961 census only two per cent of the people failed to state a religion. In a million and a half population today, approximately one million claim to be Protestant and one half million Catholic. While church attendance is a difficult factor to measure and most available surveys are ten or more years old, it definitely runs much higher than in England or the United States, with Catholics running near 90 per cent and Protestants running around 45 per cent.

Social pressure to be part of a church and to take part in church activities is strong. Sunday is still a day of rest and refraining from secular amusements and commerce, at least for the Protestant community.

I went to Northern Ireland because I suspected that the picture which we in North America received through our news is, while accurate, only a partial picture. I had reason to believe there were untold stories behind the violent headlines. I went looking for rays of hope. And it didn't take long to find Christians who have risen above the conflict, who are trying to overcome the traditions of bitterness, who are chipping away at the wall and reaching through the cracks to touch the hands and hearts of men and women on the other side. In fact, you might say that's what I found — the other side of Ireland.

Captives of History

CHAPTER TWO

Captives of History

F EW PEOPLE LIVE WITH THEIR HISTORY day by day as the Irish do. Winston Churchill wrote about Northern Ireland that "the integrity of their quarrel is one of the few institutions that has been unaltered in the cataclysm which has swept over the world."

Slogans from seventeenth century battles are today's graffiti on the ghetto walls. Politicans invoke the names of seventeenth and eighteenth century figures and repeat their arguments. Folk songs include lines such as "It seems like only yesterday to the folks of Sandy Row" and "Think on King William and the Boyne, on Cooke and Hanna, too. The grace of God has touched this shore and brought us safely through." John F. Kennedy remarked about Ireland that "what happened five hundred or a thousand years ago is as yesterday."

Not only are today's troubles firmly rooted in the past, but both sides continually look backward. The battles, treaties, dates and acts of yesterday strongly influence the outcome of events tomorrow. That's why the present conflict defies even a semblance of understanding without an insight into history.

A good place to begin unraveling the threads is with Pope Adrian IV. He was the only English pope, and in his few years of power he granted lordship of Ireland to King Henry II of England.

Henry (who is also known for the brutal murder of Thomas a' Becket at Canterbury) took an army to Ireland in 1171, but he wasn't satisfied there with recognition as king. He defied the social and political structure of the country and made his own feudal land grants, beginning the struggle between the two islands which continues to this day.

The development of the church, of course, has been one of the major themes in Irish history. Historian Arnold Toynbee points out that the real center of culture in Europe for five or six hundred years before Henry II, had been Ireland, and this culture centered around the church. For five centuries the Irish imparted culture, and England and the continent received it.

The Irish church, while confessing allegiance to Rome, tended to go its own way. Time and time again, therefore, Rome favored the English against the Irish.

When the Anglo-Norman invasion of Ireland began in the twelfth century, it had the tacit support of Rome. This, of course, was before the Reformation. For the next 500 years English kings tried to control and rule the rebellious Irish people and to stamp out Irish culture, including law, dress, names and language.

The Anglo-Irish Wars, as they are known, finally polarized around religion, and the former alliance reversed. As the Reformation took hold in England, and the English tried to reform the Irish church, Roman Catholicism became sentimentally linked to the Irish cause.

The Irish Earl Hugh O'Neill offered the last act of rebellion during that period and was defeated by Elizabeth I's military leader, Lord Mountjoy in 1603.

Perhaps no other event has affected the history of Ireland — including the present troubles — more than the plantations. Part of the English attempt to control and anglicize Ireland during the long bitter wars included the planting of English settlers. The native population was uprooted, and the land was given to loyal Englishmen who allowed the original owners to live there as tenants.

At first the plantations did not take root in the North where the great Gaelic chieftains ruled Ulster, much as they had for a thousand years. But with the military victory of Mountjoy, the last of the Irish lords fled to the continent, and their lands were declared forfeit to the crown.

In the early seventeenth century the plantations began in earnest as the final solution to the Irish problem. These lands in the North were given to settlers from England and Scotland — all of whom were loyal Protestants. The Scots were generally Presbyterians and the English identified with the Church of England.

Thus the religious lines were drawn the same as the political lines. The colonists were Protestants. The natives were Roman Catholics. And the cause of Irish freedom from that point on became solidly identified with the cause of Catholicism. The stage was then set for the next three centuries of religious/political struggle.

Taking the island as a whole, the Protestants were a minority. They were a majority in the North, but they had achieved that majority, as well as their economic superiority, by force, and they soon developed the siege mentality which exists today. The colonists lived with the expectation of uprising from the dispossessed peasants and it came in 1641. What is known as Cromwell's revenge came in 1652, and it is impossible to understand the intensity of feeling in the current struggle without knowledge of what happened on those two occasions.

The native uprising was led by an O'Neill, a nephew of the last great Ulster chieftain whom Mountjoy had defeated. It soon spread across the entire island and was fed with arms and money by Catholic powers on the continent. Thousands of Protestants were massacred. It was a brutal struggle and the plantations were almost wiped out.

Finally Oliver Cromwell arrived on the scene. He had won his struggle with the Catholic-leaning Charles I and was now the ruler of England. The Irish had generally supported Charles and Cromwell did not forget it. He and his troops marched mercilessly through the country killing thousands, looting, raping and murdering. It was a rampage inspired by ideology. Cromwell's men believed the rebels were damned, utterly wicked, and it was their duty to exterminate them. The crimes of Cromwell and his army still live in the folk mythology of Ireland today.

When Cromwell returned to England, his policies solidified the hatred and even further widened the gap between the Irish and the English. A massive physical transportation of the Irish to the counties west of the Shannon River left the land open for new plantations of more English. What few Catholics were left were landless laborers; Roman Catholic churches were destroyed and priests outlawed. Priests were worth five pounds a head to bounty hunters (the same price as for wolves).

The next significant event in Ulster history, and one perhaps more than any other that helps explain the mentality of modern Protestants, was the siege of Londonderry in 1689. Parliament had given James II the boot because of his Catholic sympathies and he fled to Ireland. There he picked up support from the Dublin Parliament, as well as an army, and he made a bid for power. But in Ulster he met fierce resistance. As James' army approached the walled city of Londonderry, the city hung in indecision. Finally, 13 apprentice boys rushed to the gates and slammed them in the face of oncoming troops. For 105 days the besieged city held out until a Protestant force from England relieved them.

The event is celebrated on August 12 every year with a parade through Londonderry. The sober-faced, bowler-hatted Protestants beat giant drums, wave banners and march on the ancient walls, flaunting the victory in the faces of the citizens in the Catholic ghetto below.

A year after the siege, the Protestant William, Prince of Orange, who had overthrown James II, landed in Ireland and defeated James once and for all at the River Boyne. This event is celebrated with a similar march every July 12, and both marches have produced the sparks that have set the tinder box of Ireland to flame many times in the last two centuries.

Now the bony thumb of John Bull held all of Ireland in misery. Less than 15 per cent of the property in the country was in the hands of Catholics. Catholics were stripped of rights, and the infamous penal laws kept Catholics and Catholicism from any political power. (Strangely enough, the laws were also used against dissident Presbyterians, descendants of Scots, whose allegiance to Britain was not always certain.)

For the next 200 years the tragedy continued, and throughout the nineteenth century, famine, rebellion, militant Protestantism and deeper animosities marked the scene.

Take this description of life in Belfast in 1872, for example: "One Sunday morning, 17 August, the streets around Millfield, the Pound, Shankill Road and Falls Road were in a state of utter desolation . . . everywhere pavements were torn up, in the streets barricades were erected and shops boarded up against attacks. In every street which bordered on the Catholic and Protestant district, pickets of armed police and soldiers stood guard. . . ." That description could easily have been written any number of times over the years, including 1975.

Various revolutionary groups such as the Irish Republican Brotherhood and the Fenian Brotherhood in America continued to feed the fires of independence. The great famine of the 1840's indirectly contributed to the rebellion. While perhaps a million people died of starvation, another million emigrated, mostly to America. Many of these picked up the struggle for independence in the new land and were able to affect the course of events back home.

When Gladstone, as prime minister of England, pushed for home rule for all of Ireland in the late 1800's, he both united and enraged the Ulster Protestants. They signed a covenant, declaring their desire to be part of Great Britain, and sectarian riots became part of the pattern of life.

As a direct reaction to Gladstone's efforts, the Protestant Orange Order grew to be a powerful religious-political organization. Anti-Catholicism and loyalty to Great Britain were more important requisites for membership than the Christian virtues which were espoused. Almost every Unionist party politician belonged to the Orange Order, and the Unionists have been the only party in power during those years.

Home rule was inevitably passed just before World War I, but Irish Nationalist leaders consented to delaying it until the war was over. The famous Easter uprising of 1916 was the act

15

of Irish Nationalists who opposed the delay. Finally, after several years of civil war and political maneuvering, England agreed to a separate Parliament for the Irish Free State in the South, and the six counties that make up Northern Ireland in the North. Eventually the South, with its majority of Catholics, embarked on complete self-government while the Parliament at Stormont in the North began in 1921 to conduct its internal affairs as part of Great Britain, much as our American states do within our federal government.

The next 50 years of a Protestant-dominated, Unionist party government in Northern Ireland were marked by sporadic violence, discriminatory legislation, careful cultivation of the siege mentality of Protestants and the strengthening of Protestant supremacy. The IRA, which rose out of the civil war, continued its arms raids and occasional bridge bombings long after it was outlawed in both the North and the South. Protestant paramilitary groups on the other side carried on similar shenanigans and occasional political murder. But by 1968, the IRA was a paper tiger, its support from the Catholic community gone and its last campaign against Ulster history.

IMPORTANT HISTORICAL DATES

1610   Beginning of plantation of Ulster

1690   Defeat of James II (Catholic) in Battle of Boyne by William II (Protestant)

1801   Act of Union—United Ireland and Great Britain in one United Kingdom

1920   Government of Ireland Act—Established independent Parliaments for south and north

1921   First Parliament of Northern Ireland opened by King George V

1921   Irish Free State established as a self governing body comprising the provinces of Munster, Leinster, and Connaught

1937   Irish Free State became the Republic of Ireland

1936   Constitutional amendment in Irish Free State removed king from all internal authority

1641   Catholic uprising and massacre of Protestant settlers

1649   Cromwell, in retaliation, massacres Catholics and confiscates land

1718   Beginning of emigration of some 200,000 Scotch Irish to America

1880   Home Rule for Ireland becomes a major issue in British and Irish politics

1937   Constitution of Republic of Ireland affirms claims to the "lost counties of Ulster."

1949   Ireland Act by British Parliament pledges ". . . in no event will Northern Ireland or any part thereof cease to be a part

17

of . . . the United Kingdom without the consent of the Parliament of Northern Ireland."

1960   Rev. Ian Paisley organizes demonstrations against "Romeward" trend in Presbyterian Church.

1968   Northern Ireland Civil Rights Association sponsors illegal march in Londonderry. RUC reaction results in riots and 77 injuries.

1969   JANUARY—Civil Rights march from Belfast to Londonderry results in clash between marchers and Protestant extremists. Television coverage brings situations to world attention.

      AUGUST—Protestant-Catholic riots result in British troops being brought into the conflict. From here the situation rapidly deteriorates.

In the next few years mass arrests are made and suspects jailed without trial; the Northern Ireland Parliament is suspended; bombings and killings escalate; business and social life are severely restricted and political chaos ensues.

Ian Paisley

CHAPTER THREE

Ian Paisley

As THE SIXTIES GREW TO MATURITY in Ireland, a climate for progress settled on the island, perhaps for the first time in 50 years. Ulster mills were working to capacity; 50,000 new jobs had been created since the war; the value of agricultural products had increased more than seven times in that period; and Northern Ireland received some 200 million pounds of direct and indirect subsidies from England each year.

It is ironic that when civil rights demonstrations broke out in 1968, Protestant/Catholic relations were slowly getting better. Things had come so far that Prime Minister Terence O'Neill felt free to invite the prime minister of the Republic of Ireland, Sean Lemass, for a conference with the new Catholic leadership. O'Neill recognized the inequities that existed within the country and his government was making some progress in righting wrongs.

But it was too little, too late for the young activists at the university. And for the right-wing, hard-core Unionist followers, it was too much, too soon. They met in a history-making clash on Saturday, October 5, 1968, in Londonderry. A TV cameraman from the Republic of Ireland filmed the police as they brutally broke up a civil rights march, and TV screens around the world carried the story.

Five years after the historic meeting between O'Neill and Lemass, O'Neill's policies were in shambles and he had resigned. British troops patrolled the streets. The state was at war with it-

21

self, and the clock of progress had been turned back hundreds of years. The tinder box was on fire again, and a new, sorry chapter in Northern Ireland's history had begun.

Perhaps no man can claim more credit for this reversal than the moderator of the Free Presbyterian Church and pastor of the Martyrs Memorial Free Presbyterian Church, the Rev. Ian R. K. Paisley.

Paisley has been called "God's man for the hour . . . the shrewdest political operator in Northern Ireland . . . a figure right out of the seventeenth century . . . a warmhearted minister and family man." His enemies take special note of his native intelligence. Bernadette Devlin,* the young civil rights worker, conceded that "in a blinkered way he is quite right." In an interview in his study Paisley told me that "I am primarily a preacher of the Gospel. A person has only to look at the work which I lead to know that that's true."

Who is this extraordinary man who has gained center stage in Northern Ireland today? How did he get there? And what part does he play in the spiritual life of the country?

No book about Christians in Northern Ireland (or any other aspect of the state) can ignore him. Toward the beginning of the civil rights marches in 1969, Bernadette Devlin made a highly unusual call on Ian Paisley in his home. They sat in his front room balancing cups of tea and chatting about children as well as politics. She found the private Paisley a warm man with a deeper intellectual grasp than usually credited to him.

Physically, Ian Paisley is a large, barrel-chested, rocky-faced man with a vibrant voice. Conor Cruise O'Brien, the Irish intellectual and a leading member of the Labor party, calls him "a symbol of the besieged Ulster fortress" and others note his computer-like command of the Scriptures.

Paisley is the son of a Baptist minister from Ballymena. He attended a technical college as well as a school of evangelism in Wales and the Theological Hall of the Reformed Presbyterian Church in Belfast. He was ordained by his father when he was

---

*Now Bernadette Devlin McAliskey

22

19 and set out to begin an evangelistic mission to the shipyard
workers.

In 1951 he was involved in a dispute in a Presbyterian Church
in the County Down village of Crossgar and led the conservative
faction out to begin a new church which he called the Free Presbyterian Church of Ulster. It was the beginning of a fast growing movement which now claims more than 30 churches.

As Paisley's ministry grew in Ulster, so did his notoriety as
the leader of the anti-Catholic, anti-ecumenical forces. He continually warred against a "Romeward trend," referring to the
pope as "Mr. Red Sox" and the Roman Catholic Church as the
"scarlet whore of Rome" and proclaimed a great battle of biblical Protestants against popery. His party paper, *The Protestant
Telegraph,* ran items such as this paraphrase of Onward Christian
soldiers:

> Onward Christian soldiers,
>   Marching unto Rome,
> Where a smiling Pontiff
>   Bids us 'welcome home.'
> Our enchanted 'bishops'
>   Lead the steady flow,
> Forward to St. Peter's
>   See their banners go.
>
> Methodists may perish
>   Wesley call in vain.
> Martin Luther's doctrine
>   Is surely on the wane.
> Cranmer, Ridley, Latimer,
>   Let them all 'get lost'
> On! to Lourdes and Fatima
>   Counting not the cost!

Paisley and his supporters packed an open air rally of a
prominent Methodist evangelist, Dr. Donald Soper, in 1959 and
harassed the man off the platform. Finally the police escorted

Soper to safety and Paisley was fined for causing a breach of the peace.

He made headlines again in June, 1966, when he led a demonstration in Belfast. His procession planned to march through a Roman Catholic area, the Cromac Square, as part of a protest against the "Romeward trend of Presbyterianism." Since the terrible riots of 1935, Cromac Square had been off limits to any Protestant march. A riot followed as the marchers came through the area but there were no serious incidents. Paisley was fined for his part in the riots, then jailed for three months when he refused to pay the fine.

When the civil rights marches began in late 1968, Paisley began organizing counter demonstrations. A march by the civil rights people in Londonderry came off as a model of nonviolence even though Protestant marchers threw stones, bottles, bricks and flour at the marchers. When another march was announced for November 30 in Armagh, Paisley complained to the Royal Ulster Constabulary that they had lost control of the crowd in Londonderry and that if they didn't stop the Armagh march, he intended to do the job.

About 1:30 a.m. on November 30, Paisley and some of his followers arrived in Armagh and stood around until dawn. He informed the police they were going to hold a religious meeting. By early morning some 1,000 men and women gathered in the Paisley group intent on preventing the civil rights group from marching. The RUC then asked the civil rights people to call off their march and avert what would certainly be a clash. Reluctantly and with some difficulty they did. (The police had confiscated more than 200 weapons, including a few guns, from the group of people which Paisley led that morning.)

The next Paisley interference with a legal march came on January 3, 1969. The Peoples' Democracy planned a three-day march from Belfast to Londonderry to begin on New Year's Day. For the first two days the police continually rerouted the marchers, claiming that hostile crowds were in the road ahead. Closer examination found none. At one point the marchers linked arms and pushed through a cordon of police blocking the road.

Meanwhile, Ian Paisley had gone to the Minister for Home Affairs and urged him to ban the last stage of the march. Failing that he organized a prayer meeting in the Guildhall in Londonderry the night of January 3. While the marchers slept under guard only eight miles from the city, a riot broke out in the Guildhall Square. Major Bunting, a close associate of Ian Paisley, told the crowd to prepare to defend themselves. The police finally broke it up but not before Bunting urged the people to meet at a church near the Burntollet Bridge the next morning. The marchers were scheduled to arrive at the bridge to the city by late morning.

Bernadette Devlin was in the front row of the marchers as they approached Londonderry the next morning and she described the scene in her book *The Price of My Soul:* ". . . from lanes at each side of the road a curtain of bricks and boulders and bottles brought the march to a halt. From the lanes burst hordes of screaming people wielding planks of wood, bottles, laths, iron bars, crowbars, cudgels studded with nails. . . ." No one was killed but 87 marchers were taken to the hospital.

Months later the Cameron Commission, a government appointed body which investigated the incident reported:

"In the face of mass evidence from both police and civilian sources as to the extent to which the supporters of Dr. Paisley and Major Bunting were armed at Armagh . . . and on the march to Londonderry, it is idle to pretend that these were peaceful, directed protest meetings.

"We are left in no doubt that the interventions of Dr. Paisley and Major Bunting . . . were not designed merely to register a peaceful protest against those engaged in civil rights or Peoples' Democracy activities . . . their true purpose was either to cause a legal prohibition of the proposed . . . demonstrations . . . or, if this move failed, to harass, hinder and, if possible, break up the demonstrations. . . . We can only condemn as an act of the greatest irresponsibility the decision to hold a meeting of the nature of that conducted by Dr. Paisley and Major Bunting in Londonderry on the 3rd of January, 1969."

The final rebuke read, "The fact remains that the police could not guarantee the physical safety of the civil rights marchers against the obvious menace of unlawful violence. For this, the actions of Dr. Paisley, Major Bunting and the associates and supporters bear direct responsibility."

A little more than a year later Paisley ran in an election for the Northern Ireland Stormont government and won. Several months after that he won a seat in Parliament at Westminster. He was then fully established as the political leader of the ultra-Protestant position and had split the 50-year-old Unionist Party.

To fully grasp the position of Rev. Ian R. K. Paisley in Northern Ireland means considering his comments and writings on various topics. This sampler comes from his sermons, from private interviews and from magazines in which he has written:

On the Roman Catholic Church . . .

"Of course the old whore of Babylon has had a facelift. Of course, she has put on the nice gloves on her bony persecuting hands. . . . Remember the tactics of Rome are unchanged. Today she seeks to reconquer our nation by papalising our Royal House of Windsor."

On Billy Graham . . .

"Billy Graham says he has the warmest relations with the World Council of Churches. Men in the World Council of Churches say that Jesus Christ is the bastard child of Joseph and Mary. He has the warmest relations with these men."

On Ecumenism . . .

"A traitor and a bridge are very much alike. They both go over to the other side."

On the Charismatic Renewal . . .

"I want to say that the charismatic movement is the movement of the false prophet leading people out to worship another Christ."

26

On Jesus People . . .

"Well I want to tell you sir, when God works in your heart, He will not only wash your heart but He will make you ready for soap and water. You will get your outside washed as well, and you will get your hair cut in a reasonable length and look respectable and decent in God's house. Let me tell you that!"

On the Irish Republican Army . . .

"The IRA is the armed wing of the Roman Catholic Church."

On Freedom and the Crown . . .

"If the forces of the British Crown are going to support the IRA to destroy Ulster, then we are prepared to do as our Fathers did and fight for our freedom. . . . When the call comes we will be able to take our stand as Protestant men in the battle that is going to be waged. . . ."

In the fall of 1969 Dr. Bob Jones, Jr., an American college president, dedicated Paisley's impressive new church on the Ravenhill Road in East Belfast. The Martyrs Memorial Free Presbyterian Church seats some 3,000 people and on an average Sunday morning may be half full. The faces of several dozen martyrs and reformation leaders ring the hall at the rear of the sanctuary. Paisley, who wrote a book called *The St. Bartholomew's Day Massacre,* seems to have an obsession with martyrdom. His magazine, for example, proclaims a new church to be for the preaching of the Gospel and *"for the defense of the Faith." The Protestant Telegraph,* a Paisley sponsored paper runs headlines such as "You are Being Watched," "Betrayal of the Faith," "Martyrs" and "Eire Plans an Invasion," all in one 12-page issue. The motto of the paper is "The Truth Shall Set You Free."

Why is this preacher of the Gospel and leader of one of the fastest growing religious groups in Ireland also playing a leading political role? "My involvement politically," he says, "is because of my involvement spiritually. People don't seem to realize it but this is a religious battle which has been fought on the political plane and the problem is not an economic problem." But mixed into the religious fervor is a patriotism which is echoed in the banner on the wall of his study, "For God and Ulster."

No matter which way the course of history goes in Northern Ireland, the Rev. Ian Paisley will most likely play a prominent part in it. While he does not represent a majority Protestant view, he does represent a sizable minority. And before peace can come, this extremely vocal and reactionary minority will have to be convinced that the threat to their way of life has been adequately overcome.

Life Under Fire

CHAPTER FOUR

Life Under Fire

T HE CLIFTONPARK BAPTIST CHURCH had been bombed, and as we drove from the pastor's house on the outskirts of Belfast, he told me how the explosion ripped out the front door of the church while the congregation sang the final hymn.

At one point we passed an armored vehicle and a half dozen British soldiers running along beside it, guns thrust out, fingers on the trigger, eyes warily searching each house or civilian or passing car. I strained to see, but the Rev. Jack Bradley didn't slow down. Nor did he stop talking. It might have been a delivery van or a bus for all he noticed.

I had been in Northern Ireland for three days and had seen the bombed-out buildings, the bricked-up houses, the side streets blocked and guarded, the army check points. I had gone through the ritualistic searching which all Belfast citizens endure as they enter the shops and offices in the center of their city. But not until I saw that pastor blithely drive on past the armed patrol did I begin to grasp the effect which six years of conflict have had on the people.

In six years the troubles have grown from a few nonviolent civil rights marches to a daily diet of bombings and shootings. More than 1,200 people have been killed. Several thousand have been burned or chased out of their homes. Some 1,500 have been arrested and jailed without trial.

A 400-foot long billboard, perhaps the longest in the world, in one of the troubled areas, carries a grim message: "Use the confidential telephone . . . if you are suspicious, dial 999 . . . don't let the bomber get your car . . . and don't let the children have toy guns." When riots broke out at the notorious Long Kesh prison, vans, trucks, and buses lay burning only a few feet away from the billboard.

It takes an hour at London's airports for baggage to be searched, then sealed in plastic bags before loading. The Belfast airport is heavily guarded and no visitors are allowed in the terminal building. The windows of the city hall are broken out and boarded up and heavy chains block the main streets. Buses passing through the center of Belfast are stopped and searched.

Armed patrols, bunkers, security checks, barbed wire, gates, double and triple locks on office buildings, shops and homes. The million and a half citizens of Northern Ireland live with a warlike tension between two communities. Except for the British troops trying vainly to keep the peace, it would be total civil war.

That's why Alec Gould was a most unlikely figure to be standing late one night in his neighbor's doorway. With a mob of drunken rioters outside, trying to burn out the Catholic family, Alec Gould, a Protestant, told them they'd have to get him first before they could get those inside.

Gould was a typical product of the Protestant society. While he lived in a mixed neighborhood, he was a comfortable part of the majority and had been brought up to keep a wary eye on all Catholics. Neighbors should get along, of course, and they were nice people. But you simply couldn't erase hundreds of years of conflict between Protestants and Catholics.

On top of that Alec Gould was still mourning his son. Sandy Gould had come home from London for a weekend, had wandered into an area of rioting and had been killed while trying to help a woman get back to her home and her children. There was no question. It was someone from the other side who had sprayed a burst of automatic gunfire that caught Sandy Gould between the eyes.

The Gould family got the news after church on Sunday and Alec Gould went into a violent rage. The pastor tried to do

32

what he could to help, finally went home and prayed for awhile, then returned. This time Alec met him at the door. His eyes were wet but he was calm. "Jimmy," he told the pastor, "God will forgive them."

The two older boys in the family went around the neighborhood urging their Protestant neighbors to leave it just as it was. "We don't want any trouble. We're praying for the people who did it. We don't have any animosities toward the Catholics. We don't want any reprisals. Let God speak through it."

But it didn't work that way. Incensed by the senseless murder and by the violence and tension that wracked the country, some of the men in the district burned down a pub, stole the liquor and began a drunken rampage. It was at this point they came to the house next to Alec Gould. Armed and in a vicious mood, they started toward the door only to meet Alec in front of them. A threat on his life didn't move him, and finally the crowd backed away into the darkness. Alec's neighbors still live beside him today.

The Alec Gould story was one of many which I heard in Ireland. Everyone knows someone who has been burned out or bombed or killed, but I found this difficult to integrate with the statistics I'd read in a recent survey. According to one of Northern Ireland's leading scientists, over the past five years you would have been considerably safer living in Northern Ireland than in any large American city. Many insist that the troubles don't really affect them much day by day. Then in the same breath they'll relate an incident such as the one I heard from a young accountant in a coffee bar.

Les lives on the south side of Belfast in a relatively unscarred area. As he shrugged off the danger and the effect which the troubles might have on him, he did allow that he couldn't take the long walks at night that he always liked to take. Then he told me of his father's business. The family had moved to a solid Loyalist area and opened up a drygoods shop. On the 12th of July, one of the Loyalist holidays, they had refused to fly the Union Jack outside the shop.

"My family have always been moderates. We didn't believe

33

in provoking the political situation and felt that history should be left back there in history."

In the following months, the Loyalist residents of the neighborhood boycotted the shop until the family was forced out of business.

All this, Les told in a resigned, "that's the nature of man" manner. No spite; no hardness. The incident had reaped a certain spiritual maturity in the young man.

Often, however, it amounts to just plain inconvenience for Christian workers, and if there is fear, they rarely talk about it. Late one night as I drove back from Londonderry to Belfast, a youth leader pointed out to me the spot where his car had broken down. It had been around midnight and he hiked to the nearest farmhouse and with some reservations knocked until the farmer opened a second story window. No, the farmer would not come down and open the door. Yes, he would call the young man's parents and tell them where he broke down and to come get him in the morning. And after he had done that, he apologized to the youth worker, hoped he'd understand and shut the window.

It was in a well-known IRA stronghold, and there was nothing else to do except go back to the car, lock the door and go to sleep. In the morning as he awoke, the police had arrived and were carefully examining the car.

While such incidents are common as well as inconvenient, they no doubt have a greater effect on the Christian than just developing patience. The tension, the awareness of danger, the closeness of it have certainly made more than one man stop to think about who he is. Les says that when he meets strangers the conversation invariably turns to the troubles, and it provides a point of beginning to talk about spiritual life.

The Royal Ulster Constabulary (the police in Northern Ireland) have come in for as much criticism during the troubles as any group in the country. If it's true any place, it's certainly true in Ulster — a policeman's lot is not a happy one. The RUC is generally not trusted by the Republicans and while the government intended to reserve one-third of its membership for Catholics, very few joined.

When the current conflict broke out, the RUC often demonstrated its bias as well as its incompetency at crowd control. Yet, among its ranks are many Christian men, trying to sort out their Christianity, their politics and their duties as policemen.

I met one of them, Ben Ford, at the Donegal Pass RUC station. You can't drive more than ten mph past the station. Humps in the road (sleeping policemen, they're called) prevent the enemy from speeding past and tossing a bomb or grenade at the door. A concrete bunker protects the policeman on guard outside the station. Fifty-gallon drums filled with concrete prevent a car or van of explosives from being rolled into the building.

I met Ben Ford in the lobby and we walked to a cafe a block and a half away. Ford is a detective, good looking, with an athletic physique and at least six or seven years older than he looks.

As we talked, he told me he had gone into that same cafe some six months earlier and ordered the patrons to leave. They had word there was a bomb in the area. Then he and his partner began to search outside.

About 30 yards from the cafe, a van stuck halfway out of an alley. Any car or van left unguarded may be suspect in Belfast and Ford and his partner approached it cautiously.

"It was unusual for a van to be sitting there, so I opened the door and got inside and saw these two boxes. I knew right away, from the smell, sort of an almond smell, that it was a bomb, and I turned around and ran." He was about eight feet away when it went off.

When Ford and I finished our coffee, we walked to the corner and he pointed out the spot where the van exploded.

"As I regained consciousness, the words of a hymn came to me:

'O love that wilt not let me go
I rest my weary soul in thee.'

Ford still limps a little, and one ear still rings and hurts. But he doesn't hurt inside. "I don't bear any animosity to any individual." It's a simple statement and you know he means it. And

35

when he takes time to travel the country as part of an evangelistic team, his Catholic co-workers willingly cover for him.

Business has been particularly hard hit. Downtown Belfast is an armed camp because the bombers have hit dozens of offices, factories, stores and restaurants.

Christian businessmen suffer the same. One group had opened a gospel record store in an arcade on North Street. When it was bombed, they came bouncing back to clean up the glass and debris and begin again. "We were heroes. They won't beat us down," they cried. The second time they just didn't come back with the same bounce. After a third bombing they closed the shop. The owners were concerned for the lives of the employees and the bomber won another round.

But the bomber doesn't always win. Three young men in Newry broke into a clothing store owned by a Christian businessman and set fire to it. They broke in by the back, however, and once they started the fire they couldn't force the front open to escape. They were trapped and burned to death. The business was a total loss but the owner went the extra mile and paid the funeral expenses of the three boys.

The price varies, but few escape some payment and many find some victory in their tribulation. Before the troubles began, two brothers in the office furniture business needed a new warehouse. They found one all right, but it was on the Falls Road in a Catholic section. Even in those days of relative calm anyone would have advised them against it. The brothers were convinced, however, that this was the Lord's will and they took the property.

When riots broke out in Belfast, they came quickly to the Falls Road. Rioters broke into the automobile showroom at the end of the block, pulled the cars into the street and set fire to the building. When the firemen arrived, the rioters harassed them and they refused to enter the building. For three days the block burned and smoldered, getting closer each hour to the warehouse stacked high with wooden desks. Each day the two brothers pleaded with the firemen to enter the block and put out the fire, but they refused. In despair they went home, tired, beaten, certain they had made fools of themselves in taking that property.

36

The next day they returned and the fire had stopped. The only bit of the block left was their warehouse. They are still there, Protestant Christian businessmen in a Catholic area where many of their friends won't even visit them.

The accountant or secretary or salesman might not run the risks of a detective like Ben Ford, but no one is ever far from danger. After six years of bombings in Belfast office buildings, one Christian described the routine as he experienced it.

"The office where I work opens at 8:30 a.m. — the workshops, stores and garages have been open and running since 8 o'clock.

"At 8:35 the Bomb Warning Alarm sounds off throughout the whole complex. On the special telephone the security officer for the day (who is one of the male staff members whose turn for this job has come round) learns that a car is parked outside the main gate with the bomber's trademark — the door open and the engine running.

"No time to lose now — get the building cleared, move personnel into the questionable security of surrounding streets. Our switchboard operator is blind — get him down the spiral staircase and away. One of our work study assistants, a Christian lad, is a paraplegic — get him down the stairs and out of the building with the timely help of a couple of colleagues.

"Round the building now, fast. Check the odd corners and places where people could be. Close the heavy fireproof doors and chalk-mark them as you go. Bring all lifts to the ground floor and switch off the power. Close down machinery, boilers, pumps, heaters, switch off lights. Don't miss anything on your check list.

"The alarm has ceased its clanging now. The building is silent, except for the sound of your own breathing and the echo of your footsteps. Along the main corridor (calling out as you go) up the staircase to the main electrical switchboard. Close the main circuit switch and move over to the little room where the special telephone sits. Look around, open the windows and doors, lift the phone and report to the nearest police station — and sit down, if you can, and wait. . . .

37

"It is now the fifth year of bombing, burning, shooting and killing. We've done this kind of thing countless times before — in the dark, wet, cold winter mornings, or the bright spring and summer mornings, or the mellow autumn mornings.

"But just now, 'Be still and know that I am God.'

"There's a battered New Testament and Psalms in my left hand jacket pocket; always the Psalms when danger is near. But this Friday morning the little book is open at Revelation 21. 'And I saw a new heaven and a new earth: for the first heaven and the first earth. . . .'

"Suddenly the world outside is in its true perspective: 'for the former things are passed away . . .' and the comfort and the knowledge of God's mercy and love in Jesus His Son is very real and very present.

"My two faithful colleagues join me with a pot of hot sweet tea and three large mugs. They shouldn't be here — I know it and they know it — but what better setting or context for a brief time of Bible reading, fellowship and prayer? We speak the simple sentence: 'Keep us, O Lord, all the day long, in Jesus' name.' They are persuaded to go — and the silence returns.

"After nearly one and a half hours the parked car is cleared by the Army Technical Officer. So, press the all clear button and pick up the threads.

"The Christian in the city is no braver, no safer and no less apprehensive than his unsaved colleagues of the working day. But he or she has the peace that passeth understanding in his heart and mind; and there is the remainder of the day to be worked and there is tomororw and next week — while Jesus tarries."

Not every Christian, perhaps, rejoices over every trial nor learns the lessons of faith in the endless testing that comes to everyone in Northern Ireland. But through the we'll-muddle-through mood of most Ulstermen you often catch the smile and the all-is-well attitude that marks the man who has more than his newspaper to turn to for encouragement.

It looked for a short time in late 1973 and early 1974 as though the politicians had worked out a tenuous agreement, at best one step toward peace and the resumption of normal life. After the Sunningdale Conference in which Westminster, the Dublin government and the major Northern Ireland political parties met, a shaky power-sharing government assumed control. Everyone held his breath. But it didn't last long. The Protestant workers groups wanted no part of what they considered a surrender and they called a general strike to bring the government down.

Schools closed; public transportation stopped; barricades went up to stop people from driving to work; electricity was cut and food supplies ran low.

Jimmy Murphy, a school teacher, businessman, preacher and a tireless Christian worker, described his reaction to it:

"Speculation as to what would happen mounted as the day approached. Many prepared early, but last minute shoppers found that supplies of bread and vegetables had already run out. Even with all the pre-publicity, thousands were taken by complete surprise when early Tuesday evening their homes suddenly plunged into darkness, the heating stopped, and the television picture shrank to a small dot as the sound faded.

" 'Candles! Where did you put the candles? Are there any matches?' I groped may way around in the darkness and eventually we had a small flickering yellow candle providing the sole light. I looked out of the window and in every home the flames threw monster shadows on the window blinds.

"At first the children enjoyed it. But as the smell of burning fat drifted through the house, the cold also settled down on us. The wise thing to do was to go to bed. So with the hot water from the tap we made a cup of tea. Nothing to eat. We must save what bread there was left for the children tomorrow.

"Upstairs the beds were cold and the electric blankets didn't work. I switched on the transistor radio and in the darkness the news announcer told us what we already knew. Large areas of the country were already in darkness. Hospitals were working on emergency power. Slowly my feet warmed up and sleep shut out the troubled world around me.

"At 1:30 a.m. I awoke with a start. Every light in the house

39

was on and there was a fire underneath me. When my head cleared I realized that the power had been reconnected and the fire on my back was the electric blanket. I rolled out of bed, went around the house switching off lights and appliances, reset the alarm and went back to sleep.

"It seemed only a few minutes later that it buzzed in my ear and called us to a one-day strike. My first reaction was 'Good!' The power is still on. Boil the kettle, make the toast, turn on the heaters, shave with the electric razor. For the next hour it was go go go. The power held just long enough to make the breakfast and my wife filled the thermos flasks with boiling water and soup.

"The caretaker from the school called to say there was no heat and the children were not to go. I got the car out and drove toward the country school where I teach. Groups of angry pickets barred the entrance to one school I passed but out in the country things seemed normal. The school buses had run but less than half the pupils turned up. Then the bus companies warned that they could not guarantee that they could get the buses back at the close of school, so we marked the rolls and sent the children home.

"We also received two ominous phone calls. No words were spoken but the message of intimidation was clearly transmitted. Later we received word that gangs were out on some roads burning the cars of those going to work.

"I left for home immediately and found a bakery shop open. I was just in time. They had also received an anonymous phone call and were about to close. They knew what would happen if they didn't.

"The power was still off when I got home so my first task was to get a good fire going. It was a beautiful winter day. The air was crisp but the sun was warm on my back as I cut the sticks we had collected on our last picnic. I stopped for a moment and surveyed the scene and the thoughts ran through my mind. They can turn off the power but they can't stop the sunshine. They can turn off the gas but they can't limit the fresh air. They can stop education but they can't keep the flowers from growing or the birds from singing. I bowed my head and praised God for His wisdom, for the night and day, the sunshine and the showers, the birds, the flowers, the air and many more things beyond the control of men. I was especially thankful to God at that moment in Belfast that His throne and His power are far beyond the reach of the intimidator."

A Bridge Over Troubled Water

CHAPTER FIVE

A Bridge Over Troubled Water

"If there were less bigoted religion in Ulster and more Christianity, there would be far less problems."
— BERNADETTE DEVLIN

QUEENS UNIVERSITY with its 5,000 students and faculty sprawls over several dozen blocks only a mile or more from the center of Belfast. The troubles began there. As a small group of university students told the Church of Ireland chaplain, "What we are aiming to do is not just to overthrow governments. We are aiming to create chaos." They did. But oddly enough the actual area around the university has remained relatively free from riots and bombings and random killings.

The Rev. Sydney Callaghan lives there on a quiet side street. He is the graying, personable, joyfully irreverent and often controversial pastor of the Donegal Square Methodist Church.

He hasn't always had it so good. For several years before the Methodist hierarchy moved him there, he lived in one of the city's toughest ghettos in the heart of the militant Loyalist area — the Shankill. Though the Shankill is considered a strong Protestant area, Callaghan insists it is primarily pagan, with not more than a third of the people affected in their day to day lives by the church.

He was assigned to the Agnes Street Methodist Church and decided that if he was going to minister to that community he

45

had to become part of it. So he moved out of the manse which was several miles away and bought a house right behind the church. Actually the thinking behind it was a lot deeper than that. Callaghan had spent a year traveling as the superintendent of evangelism for the Methodists in Ulster. It made him feel, as he put it, "a little like religious artificial fertilizer, spread thinly and evenly over the country." But it also gave him some insight into the church of Northern Ireland.

"At the end of that time it was clear to me that the church was making an impact on rural Ireland, on suburbia and on the student world. How deep, I wouldn't question, but the churches around here are well-filled on Sunday morning.

"But when I came to the ghetto and the industrial belt, I found a situation common to the rest of the world. The church was cutting little or no ice.

"What happened is that at the time of the Industrial Revolution, the church had backed the owners against the workers. It didn't bother itself too much with working-class people, with certain notable exceptions. In the main the church didn't take a stand for social justice . . . we saw people as pew fodder, as potential stars in our crown. We weren't interested in the whole man, and working-class people have not forgotten it.

"Even in large city missions which had social services there was the implication: We serve you if . . . if you send your kids to Sunday School, if you get converted (and it must be a traditional conversion with short back and sides haircut and dressing the suburban way because Jesus must have dressed like that with a bowler hat and rolled umbrella). People submitted to that sort of pressure, but when they became economically secure they said to the church, 'Get lost.' "

Callaghan saw the answer in the Incarnation of Christ. "I began to ask myself how did God get through to people. And when I looked at the New Testament there was a staggeringly simple answer — the Word became flesh and dwelt among us. When God wanted to do something about the world, He became involved with it. We emphasize the atonement today, but you can't separate the atonement from the Incarnation."

46

The reasoning was simple enough for Callaghan, but in practice it was one problem after another. When he looked at a house for sale next door to the church, he had only four pence in his pocket and the asking price was 1,000 pounds. The money materialized through friends and church members. Then there was the neighbor who swore (literally and metaphorically) she didn't want a minister living beside her. All the church wanted was people to come in and get converted and give money. Jeannie Tweedie was a forceful woman, but before long she became, Callaghan told his friends, "not only my neighbor but my defender, helper, public relations officer, taker in of messages and, above all, my friend."

One-sixty-eight Agnes Street, in the heart of the Shankill, quickly became the place to turn for help. Housing problems, out of work, bad health, need counseling — go see the Rev. Callaghan at 168. There was no office and no office hours. The door was open any time.

Young people came because one room was open to them every night as a club. The crowds grew and pushed into other areas of the house. "These young people," Callaghan reflects, "were the rejects of society. Many had been thrown out of other clubs. Much of their behavior was anti-social. They stole the records, brought in alcohol rather than drink the coffee provided and generally did so much damage that in a year the house was wrecked. Some 1,000 pounds of damage had been done and property stolen and we had to close. But not before some good relationships had been forged."

Some of the street kids began coming to church on Sunday morning but that caused problems. When they smoked and talked and chewed bubble gum the regular congregation complained, so they began a special meeting for young people with prayers and Bible readings translated into Shankilese. But Callaghan and his family still lived at 168 Agnes Street and the door stayed open and people still came.

There was, for example, "the American-Irishman who was an alcoholic and who had no friends at the end to bury him save those at our house, the man with the 'personality disorder' and the homeless baker's apprentice (subsequently married and doing well), a Canadian with a broken marriage, a Jamaican with a trail of broken relationships — and illegitimate children. There was the ex-evangelist who ran up phone bills to the continent and was released from prison by a fine being paid.

"There was the chronic gambler who said he wanted to reform but in the course of doing so wrote out some stolen checks and had to be rescued from further downfall. There was the namesake of mine who had helped but who, after release from prison, found his way to London with somebody other than his wife. There was the couple who were given accommodation who made off with an electric razor, and the ex-Borstal boy who held me prisoner for a few hours at the end of a bread knife. (Knowing of his sentence for robbery with violence, it wasn't easy to play it cool and talk him out of stabbing me.)"

Callaghan was upset when the conference moved him out of the Shankill. "It isn't that one has imagined that one was indispensable, but because of years of fighting battles and striving to be accepted first as a man and then as a minister, we felt it to be strategically wrong."

The community didn't like it either. Some 1,600 people signed a petition to protest. Jeannie Tweedie led the fight. At one house the owner balked, "I couldn't sign that. I'm a Paisleyite." To which Mrs. Tweedie replied, "I don't give a damn if you're a parasite. You will sign." Most signatures, however, were given willingly.

The appointment to Donegal Square came just about the time the troubles began and was a complete upheaval. Callaghan's student friends said he had gone from gutter to grandeur. Callaghan knew that when he went to the Shankill he had had to learn a new cultural pattern and relate his faith to it. Now it was the same process again with a middle and upper class.

But Callaghan seems to be a man who is drawn to the poor and the needy and to people who are different in some way than he is. This time he pulled some of his middle class parishioners with him to a notorious housing development on the outskirts of Belfast called Ballymurphy.

According to Callaghan, "It's a concrete jungle, a supposedly modern estate which could only have been designed by a planner with the dt's. At least he didn't have people in mind when he designed it. It's an unlit, beat-up oasis of depression. Its people are fundamentally ordinary decent folk whose religious links are with corpus Christi and whose political links would be closer to the Republican than to the Unionist tradition."

For four years now a group from the Donegal Street Methodist Church has gone to Ballymurphy at Christmastime to sing carols. Some thought they were foolish to go at first. Take a group of Protestants at night into that IRA stronghold? "Actually, it is remarkable," Callaghan commented, "that there were those willing to come. The gulf between the communities has widened so much and in an atmosphere where murder and assassination is a part of the everyday scene, it would be strange if there were not some apprehension."

But Callaghan had contacted both the local priest and commanding Army officer and the welcome mat was out. The locals provided supper for the visitors and each year the ties grew.

Callaghan describes the visit that took place one cold wet night the week before Christmas, 1973, "In spite of the weather and a small group, we were determined to maintain this gesture of good will. We had a company director who freely admits he can't sing a note and a housewife who 'just had to come.' We had a doctor of medicine and a doctor of philosophy and a young couple who brought their dog . . . a bit like McNamara's band.

"Father Desmond Wilson had prepared the faithful and the children remembered us. A group of locals guided us, helped on by some skinheads. (Their presence was possibly influenced by the presence of some of the local talent rather than a religious devotion. The girls — two of whom, between singing carols and puffing fags, assured me they wanted to become nuns — were a mixture of the sophistication of youngsters who learned the hard realities of life early and yet who have a shy adolescent self-consciousness.)"

After another visit Callaghan told about the band which the

sisters had organized to meet the Methodists and the lanterns with candles which they made for the children to carry. "Touching it was," he wrote, "to be asked by a little child, 'Father may I light my candle from yours' and to be told 'If your light goes out you can get a light from us.'"

The two groups also got involved in a joint missionary fundraising project (for a Land Rover for work in India) and the Protestants gave some assistance to a Ballymurphy self-help project.

But in Northern Ireland you don't have to go out of your own neighborhood to find people in need. And the insane shootings and bombings have not been confined to the lower class. On Saturday afternoon, December 8, 1973, Sydney Callaghan stepped out to see his good friend the greengrocer, Jim Gibson. He was a few minutes too late. Moments before, Gibson had been killed in a shoot and run incident.

That night Callaghan sat down in his anguish, and with love and anger flowing together, wrote a letter to the editor of the *Belfast Telegraph*. The paper printed it on the front page.

An open letter to a murderer . . . Dear young man, I am writing this letter to the paper in the hope that you may read it. Possibly you can't read, for there are some who would question whether somebody who would be capable of such a deed as you have committed would be intelligent enough to read.

If you can't read perhaps the friend who helped you, called in law an accomplice, might be able to read it to you for he is possibly more intelligent than you are, in that he is able to ride a motor bike and that takes a little more wit than pulling a trigger.

I am a Protestant clergyman. Along with others I have never failed to condemn violence of any sort from no matter what source it has come. That I unreservedly do again. Not, mind you, that that will mean much to you, for you are not impressed by anything we have to say.

But to keep the record straight it is spelt out again. I have also tried to serve people without regard to what their religious label may be. From the wastelands of the Shankill to the bleakness of Ballymurphy. From the deprived Falls

Road to the affluent Antrim Road, people are people and the human heart is the same no matter in whose breast it beats.

I was in Jim Gibson's shop a few minutes after you left. I wish you could have shared what took place so that you might never forget. Because you were not there I will share with you some of the memories. There are others too intimate and personal to be shared with anybody outside the family circle. At any rate Jesus did say to be careful what you did with your pearls!

As I knelt on the floor beside him, some of the blood from the wounds you had caused spilt on my hands. There was no difference between his blood and mine although he was 'one of the other sort.' But then maybe you could have seen a difference for maybe you are the sort of person who says you can recognize the difference between "our sort" and "their sort."

As I offered a prayer at the request of his pregnant wife I didn't hear a voice indicating that the God to whom I prayed was any different from the One we both worshipped in different ways Sunday after Sunday. That may surprise you — or maybe it wouldn't — as obviously you are not in touch with Him at all as otherwise you wouldn't have broken His commandment which forbids us to kill.

As we waited in the hospital while the doctors fought for his life I didn't notice any difference in the tears we shed as we prayed for strength and consolation. Neither was it any easier or the grief any less when we gathered the family together with mother and broke to them the news that Daddy was dead.

As you are so strong and courageous why didn't you wait around to do this task yourself? Was it because you couldn't have borne what we had to bear or because, like a wild beast having attacked his prey, you had gone off into your lair? What sort of person are you?

You may pride yourself on your courage but it has no significance when placed alongside Mrs. Gibson's. She carried herself with fortitude and by her strength gave her family resolution. She has no hatred in her heart towards you. She is sorry for you. Your actions reveal the depth of human depravity.

Her attitude reveals the measure of her Christian charity. She is bewildered but not bitter. You must be bitter and

51

mixed up. We both tried to pray for you but it seemed to come easier to her which is a tribute to her spirit. It came harder to me for I was angry with a passionate anger. Perhaps I can now understand more fully how Jesus must have felt when He drove the money changers out of the Temple.

Maybe it is wrong for me to feel angry with you for after all you are in part but a product of our sick society. Maybe the anger should be directed towards parents who teach their children to think in terms of "them and us" and who nurture them in bigotry.

Maybe the anger should be directed towards education systems which divide and which emphasize a history which recognizes 1690 but not 1798, which eulogizes 1912 but despises 1916. Maybe the anger should be directed at Churchmen who think in terms of narrow church structures but who are out of touch with One who taught to love our enemies.

Maybe the anger should be directed at politicians who bandy about words in public which incite to anger but who feather their own nests from the divisions which they help to perpetuate. Maybe the anger should be directed towards a society which is content to let things be with a disregard for the common humanity which binds us all together.

Maybe the anger should be directed towards myself as a guilty reaction towards having done so little to make a community where all men shall be free to worship as their conscience dictates, are fulfilled in accord with their own abilities, and are encouraged to have their aspirations realized.

While it is right that we should try to understand, nevertheless I must remind you that you are guilty and you bear personal responsibility for what you have done. I hope you are brought to justice. If not, and in the meantime, you will have to live with your own conscience. Through the long nights you will hear the sobs of broken-hearted people.

When you are being commended for your brave action you will hear another voice which condemns your wickedness. When your mind can no longer bear the torture of what you have done you will realize there is a justice written into the universe which cannot be tampered with and which has nothing to do with being caught and tried before men. Then perhaps you will realize that 'God is not mocked: for whatsoever a man soweth, that shall he also reap.'

Your possible penitence then will be too late to bring

back a man who was a good husband, a loving father, and a decent citizen whose only possible offense was that he was not identified with your group.

If there are others like you, then there are many of us who would say: If you cannot deal with your grievances in a mature and democratic way will you leave the rest of us to get on with learning to live together?

Otherwise we might die together and we would not want to be even found dead in your company.

It is hard to believe God loves you. But He does. It is hard to accept Christ died for you. But He did. Maybe if you would realize that and the implications of it for us all you might "come to yourself" and discover His way for this province. Any other way leads to ultimate disaster.

Yours in Christian charity,

W. SYDNEY CALLAGHAN.

A Day in the Life of a Child

CHAPTER SIX

A Day in the Life of a Child

In 1973 a schoolgirl in Northern Ireland won a poetry contest by writing:

Ten little soldier men standing in line.
A sniper came and shot one and then there were nine.

Nine would-be statesmen working very late.
One had his car blown up and then there were eight.

Eight youthful choristers singing songs to Heaven.
One was hit by flying glass and then there were seven.

Seven with-it schoolgirls looking round for kicks.
One got a big surprise and then there were six.

Six loyal policemen hoping to survive.
A bullet hit one in the back and then there were five.

Five busy housewives shopping in a store.
One picked a parcel up and then there were four.

Four Long Kesh prisoners longing to be free.
One made his getaway and then there were three.

Three old-age pensioners with nothing much to do.
One went to Coleraine and then there were two.

Two happy "pub-crawlers" having lots of fun.
Bombs went off behind the bar and then there was one.

One worker wondering when the war would cease.
A booby-trap exploded and then there was peace.

Irish Times, Dec. 19, 1973

Perhaps the most tragic aspect of the conflict in Northern
Ireland is the effect it has on youth. Brought up in strictly sectarian communities, educated in religiously segregated schools,
conditioned by bombings and shootings and talk of reprisals
and fear for their own lives, brainwashed by biased history lessons and hardened churchmen and politicians, caught in a self-
perpetuating system of bigotry and violence, they have little
chance to rise above it.

There have been studies of the effects of violence on children
in Belfast and they show marked abnormalities. The average
home in Northern Ireland, according to some writers, is not the
nest of love and affection it should be. In a society where differences are seldom reasoned out, but fought, beatings in the
home are common. The husband takes it out on the wife and
she turns on the children. Cramped housing certainly is one
contributing cause. Another is the continual absence of the
father. He is, perhaps, in jail or on the run or in England trying
to earn enough to send back to a hungry family, or just out in
the local pub. Mothers crack under the pressure. For years
thousands of children have lain in their beds at night listening
to the echo of gunfire and estimating the size and closeness of
petrol bombs. Boys are over-aggressive and even when evacuated
to peaceful areas they can't respond normally to anyone in a
uniform.

"The girls have nightmares. Their vivid memories are of
doors burst open in the middle of the night, soldiers with blackened faces shining lights on them and tossing them from their
bed in order to bayonet the mattress and rip up the floorboards
in search of arms."

Children throw rocks at patrols and play in deserted or burnt-out homes. One group of children sent out from a riot area into a tranquil country estate refused to play the traditional games such as soccer and track. Instead they built a mock British armored car and pelted it with rocks. Tests of children evacuated from Belfast's schools showed those who once had excellent grade school records were now two years behind their age group.

If the home offers little chance for normal development, the school is often no better. There are public and private schools in Northern Ireland, and all but a handful of Catholic children attend private Catholic schools. The public schools are Protestant dominated and both types of schools breed generations of bigots. Until they reach university or technical school, Catholic and Protestant young people have little chance to mix and develop normal social relationships.

Catholic schools generally refuse to fly the Union Jack (the British flag and thus the flag of Northern Ireland) or to sing the national anthem. In 1972 when all other schools (including Catholic) in England, Scotland and Wales closed for the anniversary of the Queen's coronation, the Catholic schools in Northern Ireland refused to close. Bernadette Devlin recalls that her high school was militantly Republican with everything Irish-oriented.

The public schools incorporate religious education classes which would offend Catholics at many points. While the government claims it is non-sectarian, a writer for the Americans United for Separation of Church and State labeled it as leaning strongly toward Reformation theology.

History, of course, is another area in which courses vary considerably from Catholic to public schools. Catholic children receive a typical Irish-eye's view of events and Protestants get the British version.

Surveys, strangely enough, indicate that more than half of the people in Northern Ireland favor integrated schools. Most see separate systems as at least one cause of the problems. Psychiatrists have been outspoken about the detrimental results of it. Even political leaders and education ministers have commented on the system as tragic.

Opposition comes mostly from the Catholic Church. Leaders rightly refer to the unwelcome reception that Catholic children would find in public schools, but they are obviously more concerned with losing influence. Canon law of the Roman Catholic Church today reads that "All the Faithful shall be so educated from childhood, that not only shall nothing contrary to the Catholic religion and good morals be taught them, but religious and moral education shall have the principal place."

Bishop Cahal Daly, one of the more outspoken Catholic clergy, vehemently denies that separate schools "foster community bitterness," and implies that mixed education would not necessarily lead to greater cooperation but greater discord as the two groups learn more about each other.

They have little chance of that, as the system is. They have more chance to learn ditties such as that which Protestant children repeat:

> "Now down on the Falls
> Where the Papishes dwell.
> To hell with their chapels,
> Their priests as well."

Catholic students blocks away pour gasoline into milk bottles for molotov cocktails while they sing:

> "Burn, burn, burn the soldiers,
> Burn, burn, burn the soldiers,
> Burn, burn, burn the soldiers,
> Early in the morning."

Rioting came to the Shankill early in the troubles, much as it had many times in the past several hundred years. The violence touched the lives of four particular young men who grew up in its narrow streets, respectable sons of Protestant working men.

60

Kevin Hamilton, Ken Smith, William Moore and Brian Russell* came from similar homes. These were the four room (two up; two down) 70 or 80-year-old affairs that form endless rows on each side of the ghetto streets. The front door of each leads directly onto the sidewalk. The area behind holds a coalbin and a toilet. There is no garden or yard in front or back.

A small coal fire provides the only heat in the house but a gas heater above the sink supplies hot water. There is no bath nor washer but there is a small refrigerator and a television.

The boys were about 15 or 16 when the troubles began this time. Then it seemed as though the long-feared Republican take-over had finally come. The history which was written in graphite on their ghetto walls and doors came alive and they became defenders of both the faith and their country. It was the siege of Londonderry or the civil war of the twenties all over again.

There was no escape from it. At home they watched guns and ammunition pass quietly from hand to hand. A knock at the door on pay day meant someone collecting for the Ulster Defense Association or the Ulster Volunteer Force. They and their friends sold orange pins on the street to raise money for the groups and they delivered door-to-door the innumerable pamphlets and papers churned out by underground presses.

Kevin soon found the action he wanted with the Tartan Gangs. On one occasion, he and his friends were assigned the job of protecting the loyal Orangemen who were marching down the Springfield Road. The road is on the edge of a Catholic area and a barrage of stones, bricks, and bottles came from the alleys. That was only a diversion, however, for blocks away the Catholics were launching a major attack on a Protestant area. The Tartan boys ran up there as soon as they got the word. As Kevin arrived, the man in front of him fell with a bullet in him. Then another one fell beside him. For the next hour he threw anything he could get his hands on at the offenders until the police charged en masse and got between the two groups.

About the same time, Ken Smith, William Moore and Brian

---

*Names, dates and some details have been changed to protect the identity of these men.

61

Russell were recruited by the Ulster Defense Association, one of the Protestant paramilitary groups which came back into strength at that time, and they spent long hours after work and on weekends drilling, studying guerilla tactics and receiving indoctrination. They also helped to build barricades in their neighborhood and to man them against the IRA hit-and-run gunmen.

One night in the summer of 1973, Smith, Moore and Russell were given a piece of paper with the name and telephone number of two attorneys. They were also given a revolver, a clip full of ammunition and the keys to a white Cortina.

At about 1:45 a.m. they were cruising the streets around the Unity Flats area near the bottom of the Shankill Road when they spotted a young man about their own age. Robert Paul Matthews heard the car behind him and turned his head when the first bullet hit him. Seconds later he lay on the pavement, bleeding from eight bullet wounds fired at point blank range.

Almost every day for a year or more the Belfast papers had reported incidents such as this one. Often they were buried on inside pages. Sometimes, a few days or weeks later the police might turn up the killer. Generally the incidents became part of a long list of unsolved senseless murders.

This case was different. For one thing, Robert Paul Matthews didn't die. A passing army patrol heard the shots and within minutes Matthews was on his way to the hospital. The same patrol alerted others who quickly spotted the white Cortina. The three UDA men had less than a mile to go to safety but they were apprehended before they could ditch the car and get off the street.

In the succeeding months they appeared for successive hearings and a trial, each time wearing UDA badges. Fellow UDA members attended the sessions and stood, saluting Smith, Moore and Russell as they left the court. The three pleaded guilty but to their comrades they were not criminals. They were heroes, soldiers defending an embattled community.

Kevin Hamilton's story ends differently. While Smith, Moore and Russell were going through their court hearings, Kevin was dating a girl from the Shankill. One Sunday night he felt an urge to go to church. He couldn't explain it, but his girlfriend didn't like it. She was incredulous and reminded him that the Tartan gang wouldn't like it. She left and he went anyway.

That night the preacher talked about the Second Coming of Christ and Kevin wondered where he would be when He came. In a moment his whole life passed before him and before that evening ended Kevin Hamilton had given his life to Christ.

Unlike many young men who want to break with the Tartan Gangs and groups such as the UDA, Kevin, for some unknown reason, had no problem. For most it means a knee cap shot off or a beating or possibly both. Kevin Hamilton, however, was soon caught up in a different kind of life. He had always wanted to be a musician so now he dragged out his guitar, and began to play and write his own songs about his new Christian life. He got into the coffee bar circuit and night after night and weekends traveled Northern Ireland singing, telling his own story and witnessing to young people with many of the same problems he had.

Kevin's conversion resembles that of hundreds of young people in any country you might name. At one moment they're defeated by the world around them, striking out in hostility and frustration wherever they can land a blow. The next moment they find freedom through the Gospel and the power of Jesus Christ in their lives and their world changes. In the case of many young people in Northern Ireland today, conversion has brought a recognition of the tradition of bitterness in which they have been steeped for years. Kevin and others told me that they struggle with it. It isn't something they can simply put behind them and forget. It's often difficult to really love people from the other side. So they pray about it, and ask God to deal with it in their lives.

The most exciting Christian work and testimony that I witnessed all over the country came from young people. The openness to the leading of the Holy Spirit on the part of youth cuts across denominational lines and in fact erases them in most cases.

The same restlessness and uneasy activism that drove some into senseless violence gripped many Christian young people with different results. On the north side of Belfast a small Brethren assembly struggled along with a dozen or so in their youth group before the troubles began. A year or two later they had 50 or 60 involved.

Jimmy Murphy grins as he recalls the early struggles he had understanding them.

"They wanted to get out and do something, including many things I would admonish them not to do.

"For example, during the general strike there were local men with masks and guns manning barricades in our area. The young people couldn't get to work so they organized a prayer meeting and either they got tired of praying or they got motivated. Anyhow, before we knew it they had their guitars out and were preaching and singing to the men on the barricades. We thought they'd get lynched.

"They have a regular Friday night meeting in the hall and one night the paratroopers came around to check. They thought it was a dance or something. While the major in charge of the group was inside talking to the leaders for a few minutes, two of the girls slipped outside and began talking to the soldiers on the armored vehicle about Christ. As the major came out and they drove off, the girls admonished the soldiers, 'You think about it now.'

"The next Friday the major came back. 'I brought you another one,' he told the leaders laughingly. 'What do you mean?' they replied. It seems that during the week one of the soldiers had become a Christian. The major as well as other soldiers had noticed a change in him and this time the major had brought another soldier."

Jimmy smiles from ear to ear on that one. A year later he performed the wedding ceremony for that soldier and one of the girls who witnessed to him that first Friday night.

There were foxhole conversions in the group as well. Like the fellow who was playing soccer one day when a machine gunner sprayed the playing field. A dozen or so young men hit the ground and lay there as the bullets kicked up the dirt around them. This young man made a promise to God then and there if he got away alive he would give his life to the Lord. He did and his whole life changed as he got involved in the youth group.

Ballysillan Park where this youth group meets is not one of the ghetto areas where much of the rioting and shooting goes on. It is a modern housing development but few places in Northern Ireland are very far from danger. Across the street from the church hall dozens of young people hang around a milk bar and the church kids urge them into the youth hall each week.

The leaders had asked Jimmy one week to speak on the topic of love, courtship and marriage and he began speaking about twenty minutes to nine. He was supposed to stop at nine sharp but hadn't finished all he wanted to say. "Something got into me and said 'go on' so I spoke for another five minutes or so before I quit."

Just as he closed the meeting by praying, a burst of automatic gun fire broke the quiet. Jimmy was the second one out the door, behind one of the youth leaders and he stumbled in the darkness toward a bundle of clothes in the middle of the road. It was a young boy. He had been hanging around the milk bar and had been caught by the hit-and-run killers. If he had stopped preaching on time, Jimmy reflected, some 60 or 70 young people would have been out in the street milling around the milk bar as they did after the meeting each week.

In another Protestant area in Belfast the Rev. Sam Elliot came to a church where there were almost no young people. Sam is a 50-year-old, reverse collar Church of Ireland parish priest. He's a working man's pastor, a plain speaking, down-to-earth type with a penchant for frequent belly laughs and self-deprecating remarks.

One of the first things Sam did in his new church was to pray that God would give them a ministry among young people. The very next Sunday evening as Sam had just begun the sermon, the rear doors of the church flew open and with a shouting and banging, to the horror of the congregation, some 80 young people stomped in.

They were members of various Tartan gangs and there had been trouble up the street. A church was the safest sanctuary, so in they had trooped.

Sam saw it as an answer to prayer, but he was as flabber-
gasted as anyone else. He had the good sense to stop his sermon,
however, and welcome the visitors. He was even so informal as
to call attention to the scarves which were hanging around their
midriffs. That was a faux pas. Sam later learned that the plaid
scarf hanging down from each boy's waist was a gang badge.
Early in the troubles three young Scottish soldiers had been
killed and Protestant youths who wanted to get a hand in the
action along with their elders, organized and called themselves
Tartan Gangs in honor of the three soldiers. In the past several
years various gangs had slashed a teenage girl with a razor,
carved UDA on the hand of a child and raped a widow and
killed her 15-year-old imbecile son.

The rest of the service was bedlam. Sam prayed silently for
wisdom. He finally ended the meeting and then invited everyone
into the parochial hall for fellowship. Many of the adults went
home, but the Tartan boys stayed.

They not only stayed, they came back the next Sunday and
the next — not all of them, half perhaps, encouraged by Sam's
frank admission that he didn't want to change their dress, just
their lives.

Finally the night came when he was preaching, "either you
are for Christ or against Him." Tom, one of the leaders of the
gang came penitently to the front and knelt at the chancel. He
was the first of the boys to give his life to the Lord. Others followed, and their families and the community noticed. The local
probation officer came to Sam and told him, "You're making my
job easier. I can't believe the change in those boys."

Above: It has taken thousands of British soldiers and as many feet of barbed wire to keep peace in some parts of troubled Belfast.

Right: Terrorists planted so many bombs in motor vehicles that parking is severely restricted in many places in the cities.

CONTROL ZONE
NO VEHICLE
MAY BE LEFT
UNATTENDED
AT ANY TIM

*Crowds watch as British soldiers erect barricades
after a bombing incident.*

SUPPORT LAW & ORDER

THE SECURITY FORCES REGRET THE
INCONVENIENCE CAUSED BY THESE BARRIERS

UNFORTUNATELY THEY ARE ESSENTIAL
FOR PUBLIC SAFETY AND TO ASSIST
IN THE DEFEAT OF TERRORISM

In the center of Belfast, women pass through one of the many check points where their purses and packages are searched. The sign posted on the barrier proclaims the government's apology.

Searching is so commonplace for Belfast citizens that workmen have a hearty laugh at the camera.

Soldiers help clean out a deserted home, then board it up to keep out snipers.

Children in Northern Ireland often chat with armed patrols as they play in the streets around their homes.

*The building at the right,
in the center of Belfast, was burned
out by a bomb, which probably looked
something like the one at left.
Here the explosive is wrapped
in plastic, then stuffed in a
canvas sack.*

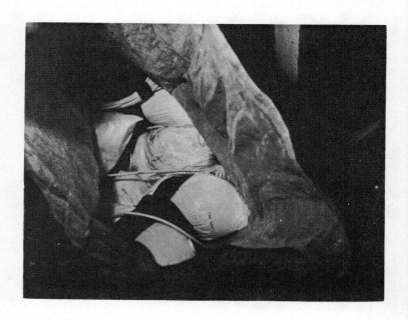

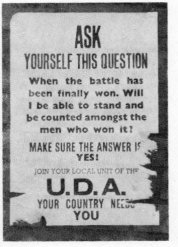

ASK
YOURSELF THIS QUESTION
When the battle has
been finally won. Will
I be able to stand and
be counted amongst the
men who won it?

MAKE SURE THE ANSWER IS
YES!

JOIN YOUR LOCAL UNIT OF THE
U.D.A.
YOUR COUNTRY NEEDS
YOU

*Protestant sections of the
cities and towns are often
papered with signs such as
the one above.*

*The UDA and the IRA are
only two of the terrorist
organizations which make
constant searches by
British troops
necessary. (Left)*

The Martyrs Memorial Free Presbyterian Church in the Ravenswood section of Belfast is the headquarters of Protestant leader and politician, the Reverend Ian R. K. Paisley.

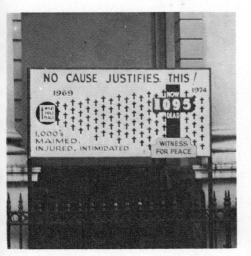

Left: This sign in front of a church greets Belfast shoppers and commuters as they board the buses in Donegal Square, in Belfast.

Below: The Abercorn Restaurant in Belfast, now rebuilt, was completely destroyed in a bomb blast, March 4, 1972, which killed three.

*British soldiers find very few minutes to relax.
Even in the half safety of an armored vehicle,
they are the target of both physical
and verbal abuse.*

The soldiers and women at the check point seem
friendly enough, but the guard inside the cement
block bunker has the barrel of his carbine out
to watch for trouble.

Right: Youngsters with play guns watch the soldiers with real ones in a Belfast street.

Below: It doesn't take much — a stray rock or a car backfiring perhaps — to send a soldier sprawling. The fighting has claimed the lives of more than 275 British troops since 1969.

Above: Soldiers and police warily check a box taken from a citizen passing a check point. Explosives in innocent-looking packages such as this have caused millions of dollars of damage.

Left: Soldiers and citizens assumed easy rapport when troops first came to Northern Ireland. Much of that has since been lost.

Right: Armored vehicles follow patrols of British soldiers down a side street in Belfast.

Below: Graffiti on the city walls proclaim a Protestant slogan.

The Gentle Revolution

CHAPTER SEVEN

The Gentle Revolution

W<small>HEN THE LEADER</small> of the Sunday night prayer meeting on
the Antrim Road invited me to attend, I jumped at the chance.
I had heard about these "mixed" meetings — groups of Catholics
and Protestants quietly gathering in various parts of the country,
praying, singing, fellowshiping together.

The only problem was getting there. I was staying in a hotel
in the university section and it meant driving across the city at
night. I had driven around Belfast during the day, often losing
my way, but generally without fear of driving into a strong
partisan sector. (You can buy published maps of Belfast which
identify each area as Catholic, Protestant or mixed.) It was
different at night. Many streets are unmarked and unlit. In some
poorer sections, entire neighborhoods are pitch black. A series
of barricades and one-way streets makes it impossible to drive
directly across the center of town. One wrong turn and you're in
a street where everyone knows you're a stranger, where you
don't belong and where, especially at night, you're not welcome.

I studied the map thoroughly before I left the hotel and
imprinted each turn on my mind. I also prayed. Through the
Donegal Pass to Cromac Street to Victoria Street, left on Great
George's and right on York Street, then left on Limestone Road.
That put me on the edge of troubled areas. Several times I wasn't
sure. Finally I saw the sign "Antrim Road" and thankfully found
the "neutral" building for the prayer meeting.

Forty people sat in a circle in an unheated room. Some of the

85

women had come across the city from Anderson's Town, a strong Catholic section. There were several nuns and only a few Protestants that night. Larry Kelly, a customs inspector, led the meeting. I sat beside him.

It went much like scores of prayer meetings I had been to at home — some weak singing of gospel songs, hesitant testimonies, occasional sharing of a few verses of Scripture and interpretation, seasons of prayer. It was informal and slow, almost stilted. Yet the Spirit of God settled on the meeting. No one noticed the cold, nor did they notice what part of town or what background the person who sat beside them came from. The wall was gone. They were simply God's people meeting together.

I told how I had sprained my ankle before I got on the plane to come to Ireland. My ankle had swollen and for several days I could barely get a shoe on. On the fourth day, conscious of the work I had to do in the next ten days, I got down on my knees and asked the Lord to heal my ankle. The next morning the swelling had subsided. Now I wanted to thank Him. That brought a spark to the meeting, and Catholics and Protestants prayed for me.

At one point while we were praying, I heard a very quiet, sort of babbling sound beside me. I turned my head and realized that Larry Kelly was praying in tongues.

This was, I had been told, a "charismatic" prayer meeting, one of the half a dozen or so in Northern Ireland and part of what is called the Irish Charismatic Renewal. While the movement is numerically stronger in the South, it is, perhaps, of greater interest as it confronts the rigid sectarianism of the North.

Pentecostal churches have been in Northern Ireland for many years. The church page in the Saturday *Belfast Telegraph* carries notices for ten or more. What is referred to as neo-pentecostalism appeared in Presbyterian and Church of Ireland circles around 1971. It began in the Catholic churches in Ireland with a small group in Dublin in 1972. In two years it burgeoned to where hundreds attended the Dublin meeting and then Protestants began to attend. Soon other meetings sprang up in the South.

The first Catholic pentecostal in Northern Ireland was, no doubt, Frank Forte. His story has been told many times.

Frank owns a cafe opposite the Europa Hotel in Belfast. Next door is a dry goods shop owned by a deacon in a pentecostal church.

For years the two men had discussed religious questions, even studied the Bible together. They both knew what it meant to trust Jesus Christ as Lord and Savior, yet their discussions bore little fruit.

Frank listened when his neighbor talked about baptism in the Spirit and found himself anxious to know if a Catholic could experience this. When he heard about American Catholic charismatics from a priest, he concluded, "It belongs to us as well as to them."

One Monday morning in 1971 Frank Forte called the pastor of an Elim church in Belfast. He had carefully read the passages in Acts 2 and I Corinthians 12 and 14 and told the pastor, "I would like to receive the baptism of the Holy Spirit."

That threw the pastor. He stalled at first. But after several meetings was convinced this was of God.

As he described the experience, "Placing my hands gently on his head, I called upon the Lord and we praised Him together. Suddenly a quiet flow of tongues issued from Frank's lips . . . the first Catholic pentecostal in Northern Ireland, I reflected in awe."

In a short time Frank prayed for a friend of his who had the same experience. Next it was Frank's son, a Belfast schoolteacher.

It was more than a personal experience, however, for the first time in who knows how long Protestant and Catholic Christians broke through the wall that separated them for a hundred years and fellowshiped together. Phillip Streeter, the pastor who prayed for Frank Forte, described the experience. "I vividly remember a certain summer evening in 1971 when, for the very first time, I realized and experienced the full significance of Christ's words uttered as He confronted His glorification. 'May they all be one. Father, may they be one in us, as you are in

87

me and I in you, so that the world may believe it was you who sent me.' (John 17: 21)

"Across the suffering city of Belfast, rioting youths were hurling bricks, petrol bombs and anything they could lay their hands on at British troops. Bullets had been raking opposing communities, and in a matter of weeks internment would be announced, resulting in a glut of violence.

"That night, however, I was one of a small group of Catholics and Protestants who had met together to pray and share in the love of Jesus. Differences? Yes, but no divisions. With arms around each other, we experienced the warm delight of happy children belonging to one Heavenly Father, baptized into one Spirit, and adoring one Savior. The mutual love and unity of Spirit invoked a spiritual renewal in my own life that night."

It was a year later, however, before a regular prayer meeting began. That was the one I attended on the Antrim Road. Then, another one began at the Priory in the small town of Benburb, an hour out of Belfast.

The best known, perhaps, and the most symbolic is one in a monastery which sits right on the peace line.

Many others, from different groups, have found unity in the movement. A former Church of Ireland chaplain at Queen's University, Cecil Kerr, commented that "charismatic shared prayer groups are an expression of grassroots ecumenism where, when people come together to pray in the power of the Holy Spirit and in the name of the Lord Jesus, and they discover a unity together that no church leaders, councils, committees could ever bring or impose, it is obviously a work of God's Holy Spirit."

If there is any one area in Northern Ireland where the sectarian walls have been toppled, where men and women on both sides are reaching across the old barriers, where traditions and bitterness and prejudice seem to have dissolved, it is in the charismatic movement.

American musicians, Jimmy and Carol Owens and Pat Boone, part of the movement in this country, saw the same thing happen in Northern Ireland. They took a group of American and British singers to Belfast to present a musical appropriately called, "Come Together," which Jimmy and Carol had written. The main point of the musical is reconciliation — healing wounds in the body of Christ — and in Belfast it met its greatest test.

They arrived at a time when there were several bombings a day and with some 50 British singers who were not on the Irish popularity list. First the newcomers had to meet with the Irish singers, mostly Protestant, but some Catholic. That came off well. The initial awkwardness disappeared and the two groups laughed and prayed and sang together in rehearsal.

What would happen when, and if, the public came was another matter. Carol Owens described what was certainly an unusual night in Belfast. The public wasn't "in the habit of lining up in the streets to attend any kind of performance. It was dangerous. It was also slow and inconvenient because everyone must be searched . . . Soon they 'queued up' around the block; a thing which hadn't happened, we were told, since the troubles began in Belfast!

"And a mixed bag they were: evangelicals, charismatics, Church of Ireland, Roman Catholic (including priests and nuns in clerical garb) and British soldiers with walkie-talkies and automatic rifles. There were even a few of Maharaj Ji's followers . . . The 1,700-seat hall filled fast and people spilled into the overflow room. About 200 were turned away."

Jimmy and Carol Owens made the introductions at the beginning of the program, and Pat Boone stood to his usual warm reception. The music began, "Come together in Jesus' name!" When the time came in the program for the audience to minister to one another, they were ready. Carol describes it again, "It was as though they had suddenly been given permission to do exactly what they wanted or what they had been secretly longing to do: to be reconciled to their born-again brothers in Christ! They were one . . . they turned to one another, many with tears, and began to share and pray."

The meeting ended with an anthem which takes its words from II Chronicles 7: 14, "If my people, which are called by my name, shall humble themselves, and pray, and seek my face, and turn from their wicked ways; then will I hear from heaven, and will forgive their sin, and will heal their land."

The Owenses and Pat Boone left Northern Ireland but "Come Together" continued. Local groups performed it in a half dozen more cities and even took it to Dublin. In each case it brought together not only Protestants and Catholics, but various Protestant groups which often would have little to do with one another. People still talked about it a year later.

Anything that will help relieve the tension is welcome in Northern Ireland, and the charismatic movement is probably accepted better by the established churches there than in many places. No doubt its appearance at a time of prolonged conflict has had something to do with it.

The question, of course, which is on the minds of everyone — inside and outside the movement — is whether it can do what the churches in Northern Ireland have failed to do, i.e., help to bring about an end to the violence.

Some obviously believe that it can. Father Jerome McCarthy, a Catholic who is deep into the movement, wrote that neo-pentecostalism "has a power and a force in it that makes much doctrinaire and bureaucratic ecumenism seem irrelevant in the face of such existentially urgent situations as . . . in the North of Ireland. . . . Perhaps there has begun a gentle revolution that by quietly changing people, irrespective of denominational loyalties, will eventually have a visible effect . . ."

Larry Kelly made a more guarded statement. "The Lord is giving us new life, new hope, new faith and a new love. In these the visionary will see the healing of our land and the bringing of our people together." He cautiously adds that "even now we can see the emergence of new political institutions as an answer to prayer." But those political institutions have had practically no effect, if any, on the situation.

Lest We Forget

CHAPTER EIGHT

Lest We Forget

MANY IRISHMEN WHO TALK LONGINGLY of revival hark back to the great revival of 1859 or to the early twenties and the ministry of W. P. Nicholson. With typical Irish inclination to look to the past, they search the grab bag of history for a reason to hope for the future. They find that in at least several situations.

When partition came to the country in 1920 and a parliament was set up in both the North and the South, civil war broke out. The Republicans wanted none of John Bull's limited form of independence. They opted for complete freedom and fought the government that was willing to live with the loose reins with which England still held the country. Michael Collins headed the new government. Eamon de Valera headed the Republicans who were opposed to the treaty with England.

The fighting, of course, spread to the North. The notorious Black and Tans shot first and asked questions later. Eight thousand armed members of the IRA crossed into Northern Ireland and used the already volatile religious divisions to bring chaos to the land. A description of Northern Ireland written a few years after, reads like one written today.

"Fear and uncertainty filled the minds of the people . . . Murder and destruction, for the time being, seemed to be on the throne . . . in those days it was with fear and trembling that one ventured on the streets. Horrible atrocities were committed and destruction of valuable property was a daily occurrence."

Into this situation came W. P. Nicholson, an evangelist who

93

had spent many years in America and was now returning to his homeland.

While few history books mention him, many Christians credit much of the subsiding of the violence to his influence. It is clear that God brought revival to Ulster through him.

Many are the stories that are told about his work. For example, the shipyards (the city's main source of employment) felt the benefits in a strange way. They had to build a new warehouse to hold all the stolen goods that were returned by their repentant employees.

Nicholson was an extraordinary man. Some described him as "most able and efficient . . . a man of extraordinary gifts, strong and attractive personality with a wonderful experience and wide knowledge of life and man." Others weren't so sure. They were offended by his "blunt methods of address" which appealed to the shipyard and mill workers.

It would be idle, his defenders conceded, "To conceal that Mr. Nicholson is criticized. Any man that comes along and stirs things up, making ordinary church-going insufficient and more rather than less a failure in its spiritual results, will find himself criticized."

What they meant to say was that Nicholson was an individualist whose often crude language and unorthodox methods attracted the thousands of shipyard and woolen mill workers. He told jokes and laughed with them, led the singing without a piano and generally offended many of the more proper church leaders. No one, however, questioned the results.

Not only the shipyards and mill workers, but cabmen, gangs on the street corner, girls from the warehouses, businessmen, students and people of leisure and wealth flocked to the meetings.

In the first three months of 1923 one periodical estimated 5,000 men and women came to Jesus Christ. Men marched in hundreds from the shipyards to the services. On one occasion so great was the pressure of men to get through the church gate that the top of one of the pillars was pushed off. Church after church testified to renewal with "mid-week prayer meetings not as formerly with ten or twenty . . . but overflowing . . . with attendances of between 300 and 400."

One of the outstanding features of the revival was the number of men converted. And the *Irish Christian Advocate* wrote, "Business people have had debts, long since written off as irrecoverable, paid in full. Money wrongfully used has been returned. At the last petty sessions court there was only one case down for trial . . ."

But the hope hidden by those who yearn for a W. P. Nicholson is expressed by some verses written about him at the time.

> "What means the curious eager throng
> That line the streets and wait so long,
> And what went ye out for to see?
> The island men in dungaree,
> Those are the men that have been won
> For Christ by Pastor Nicholson.
> Make way, make way, you hear the cry
> And let the Islandmen pass by.
>
> No bullets fly, no bombs explode,
> For Jesus leads them on the road.
> Peace is proclaimed and all is well.
> The devil has lost recruits for hell.
> Down in the dumps we'll let him go,
> And that's the place to keep him low;
> Make way, make way, you hear the cry,
> And let the Islandmen pass by."

When I visited Northern Ireland in 1969 and 1970 I heard frequent references to W. P. Nicholson and the peace-making influence of revival in the twenties. Some even harked back to the "Great Ulster Awakening of 1859" and Ian Paisley wrote a detailed history of the events. While no one has made the comparison, the climate of life in Northern Ireland at that time was not comparable to the early twenties or to today. While the seeds of revolution were being planted in the South, the North

95

was not marked by the sectarian riots it had experienced and would in the future.

The records from the church papers of the day make little or no mention of the effect of renewal on other than church life. "Nearly all our Northern circuits shared in the plenteous rain, and thousands of sinners, of every class and grade were brought to Christ," the Wesleyans reported. The Presbyterians wrote of "an immediate accession to her professed membership reckoned by many thousands" and such other benefits as "an overflowing stream of candidates for the ministry . . . a forward movement in philanthropic and missionary enterprise" and "a great increase in the sense of responsibility" of church members to active church work.

Many people continue to pray and to look continuously to this man or that, asking if he might be the one sent by God to turn the country on its ear.

When revival came to Northern Ireland the last time it came through one man on a platform preaching to the crowds on the benches before him. And the expectation of many, it seems is that revival, if it is to come again, will come in the same form and fashion.

Few within the established churches appear willing to consider the charismatic movement as the means which God might use to turn Ireland upside down in the seventies or bring an end to violence or make any significant breach in the wall which has stood for centuries. They're willing to recognize God's hand in it without recognizing that He might use it to do the very thing they have prayed for for so long.

It is within the charismatic renewal, however, that I heard people praying the type of personal "begin with me, Lord," that brings revival. It was in these groups that I heard people confess to bitterness and a need to deal with prejudice. Here I heard people say, "I haven't loved Catholics the way I should," or "I haven't loved Protestants, Lord, help me." Not a general, "I have sinned," or "I am a sinner," or "we need forgiveness," but a specific "I have discriminated against this one or on this occasion I hated these people and now I repent."

In one charismatic prayer group a Catholic girl crossed the room and knelt before a Protestant. She asked forgiveness for the bitterness she felt against Protestants and asked the girl in front of her to pray that God would remove those feelings. A Protestant had killed someone close to her. "I understand exactly how you feel," the girl in front of her replied. "My brother was killed by someone from your community."

Tearing Down the Walls

CHAPTER NINE

Tearing Down the Walls

THERE IS A SAYING in Northern Ireland, that if you can't see the mountains, it's raining. And if you can see them, that means it's going to rain.

It was raining the day I drove down the hilly, twisting roads from Belfast to Rostrevor, and the Mountains of Mourne were shrouded by heavy clouds. They are one of the most peaceful sights in Northern Ireland as they brood over the patchwork farmland to the west. To the east and to the south, they roll down to the Irish Sea and to the Carlingford Lough.

In Rostrevor I found the Christian Renewal Centre, a sprawling, slightly dilapidated stone mansion, which sits on the Northern Ireland side of the Lough looking toward the Republic of Ireland across the water.

That's symbolic. In a land of seldom-crossed-barriers, the Christian Renewal Centre draws people together. According to Cecil Kerr, the Anglican who founded the place, "In Northern Ireland it's very difficult to meet across the barriers . . . and they're not just political . . . it's sometimes as difficult for Presbyterians and Baptists to get together as it is for Roman Catholics and Protestants . . . But I find the Holy Spirit is destroying that."

Catholics in the charismatic movement say that few people in Northern Ireland have bridged gaps the way Cecil Kerr has. As the Church of Ireland's chaplain for Queen's University in the late sixties, he watched the birth of the civil rights movement

101

firsthand. He also talked to the revolutionaries. "What we're aiming to do," they told him, "is not just overthrow the government; we're aiming to create chaos."

"But what are you trying to build?" Kerr asked. "You don't have to answer that question," they told him, "until you have the chaos."

Kerr heard of the charismatic movement in America through some visitors from Houston, Texas. He was curious but cautious. Later he went to the States and spent time with the same men to learn more about it. He observed the charums, as they call them, the speaking in tongues, utterances, healing, etc. But he was more impressed by the life and work he saw among the people.

Back in Ireland he was anxious to see the same thing happen, and he began a before-breakfast Bible study with a few others in the Book of Acts. One day he asked the Lord to fill him with the Spirit and that changed his life and ministry. He then began a regular meeting in his Church of Ireland center and soon he was a leader and prime mover in the movement.

For example, Kerr brought a mixed team of Catholics and Protestants to his hometown of Enniskillen, a mixed community close to the border. The Protestant churches organizing the youth conference "allowed it." For the first time in that conference a Catholic girl from Dublin stood and told how the Lord had changed her life and what a transformation conversion had brought for her.

Kerr was a leader of the group that brought "Come Together" to Dublin. It was part of a weekend conference of some 700 or more Catholics and 400 Protestants. It was historic, according to Kerr. "Before one of the sessions the Catholic bishop from America and the Presbyterian pastor from Bangor in the North knelt side by side and prayed . . . there were Brethren, Church of Ireland, Methodists, Presbyterians and Roman Catholics in that room. It was a wider vision of what God wanted us to do. I've never worked with a group of people so committed together. They didn't just sing; they prayed. Just after the rehearsal they went around and prayed over every chair in the

102

Mansion House that God would bless the people coming to sit in those chairs. It was a remarkable weekend."

The Christian Renewal Centre was Cecil Kerr's dream. "I could have gone into a church in Belfast and developed a ministry there. I was invited to. But I felt that one of the things the Holy Spirit is saying to us in the church is that He wants to see His body manifest in this country . . . He wants to see people from every background coming to Him . . . I'm convinced that this is one thing the devil does not want to see in Ireland. . . .

"So we felt that a community of people who had been drawn together as the Lord would lead us from different backgrounds living in fellowship and prayer here would be a witness to others. . . ."

Some time ago the mansion which they took over had been divided into seven flats and walls erected to divide the flats. Kerr and his friends set out right away to take those walls down and a visitor quickly pointed out the symbolism there. "That's what we're doing in the spiritual realm. We're taking down walls that shouldn't have been there in the first place."

Many conservatives, not unexpectedly, criticize Kerr and other charismatics for their courting of Catholics. Protestants in Northern Ireland, as a rule, find it hard to accept that a Catholic can be a Christian.

One publication charged that the "charismatic gospel is devoid of repentance." Anyone who has been to a charismatic prayer meeting, however, knows better than that. The sensitivity and awareness of the leading of the Spirit brings about constant prayer for forgiveness of specific sins.

Others claim there is too much emphasis on experience and not enough on doctrine. Kerr has answers for that, too. He has obviously spent time both in study, long conversations with and careful observance of Catholics.

"I think that one thing I have learned in my contacts with Catholics who are baptized in the Spirit and really love the Lord is that their way of expressing their faith in Him will be different.

103

"For example, in 'Come Together' there is an opportunity given for people to acknowledge their faith in the Lord. After the song, 'All We Like Sheep Have Gone Astray,' anyone who wants to receive the Lord, to give their lives to Him, can come forward.

"Now what I've learned is that when you are working with a Catholic audience, if you talk to them in evangelical phraseology such as 'receive the Lord,' what comes to their minds is the sacrament and receiving the Lord in the elements of bread and wine. So if you're trying to convey what we mean by receiving the Lord, you talk about having a personal encounter with the Lord Jesus. Then they know immediately what you're talking about. So when we did 'Come Together,' in Dublin, that was the phrase I used and about 200 hands went up of people who wanted to come to the Lord as a living Person.

"What I look for isn't the phraseology. I look for the reality of their faith in the Lord as a living power and presence in them. When you see that you recognize it.

"I come from an evangelical background and I appreciate tremendously what I've received there, but I encourage my Protestant friends to keep their hearts open wide to what the Lord is doing and don't try to do the Holy Spirit's work for him. I return again and again to the passage about Peter in Cornelius' house. The Lord had to take him by the scruff of the neck and show him a vision. He didn't talk to him in theological language. Then when he came into the house of Cornelius you remember he found it very difficult to accept. They didn't have the theology straight but they had the Spirit of the Lord dwelling in them and he accepted them.

"I think this is what God is calling us to do. The theology, the understanding, the Biblical perspective will follow when people have the Spirit of God dwelling in them.

"One thing we evangelicals often do is to take over and decide that we can really do the job better than the Holy Spirit and decide how a person is going to come to the Lord and whether or not they have by the expressions they use. Pentecostals and charismatics do this too . . . this business of saying

104

you've got to speak in tongues or have an experience like mine. This is an awful danger. God who is infinite in love and mercy has created us individually. He's not going to mix us all up in the same experience.

"One of the problems is language. There are many who have the language but not the life. And there are those who haven't gotten the language but they have the life. I'd rather have the ones who have got the life without the language."

Kerr's long conversations with Catholic charismatics have generally uncovered more points of agreement than not. For example, many Protestants get stuck on the Roman Catholic doctrine of absolution. Traditionally many believe that the priest gives absolution, i.e., forgiveness of sins. "But I've had this out with a number of them," Kerr says. "And I've discovered they mean the same thing that we mean in the Church of Ireland. What they actually do is *pronounce* God's absolution when someone truly confesses sin and repents. . . . In our prayer book it says that if anyone is so troubled in their conscience that they can't find forgiveness, they should go to a minister of God's Word and find the forgiveness which God brings. Now I would say there are many Roman Catholics who have a mechanical view of confession, but the ones I know in the charismatic revival are close to us. The Archbishop speaking in Dublin said to the crowds that we come directly to the Father through what the Son has done for us and there is no need to come through any other. This is the kind of theology that's coming across in the charismatic revival."

Kerr's writings and messages often center on passages such as Ephesians 2: 14, 15 and Colossians 1: 19, 20, passages which emphasize reconciliation. Coming together, breaking down barriers, breaking down the dividing wall of hostility — these are phrases which Kerr repeats over and over again.

And certainly in his mind it's happening. There is a genuine renewal in Northern Ireland. He doesn't talk about numbers but about an event. "In answer to the faithful prayers of God's people all over the world, the Holy Spirit is moving in a new way in Ireland today."

105

Perhaps the best word picture of what is happening came from an editorial in a small magazine.

"At a prayer meeting in Queen's recently God gave us a picture which challenged and encouraged us. It was a picture of a high, cold wall — the symbol of so much division and bitterness in our land. At the base of the wall there was a little tree growing — a tender plant quietly and almost imperceptibly pushing its roots into the shallow soil at the base of the wall. A geology student who was in the company helped us to understand what God was saying to us through that picture. He explained the mightiest force on earth was the power of living tissue; it can break open the solid rock and is more powerful than steel. In time as that little tree grows it can break down those hard, cold walls of hate and division, and the new life that God abundantly provides will be shared by all."

A Flower Grows

CHAPTER TEN

A Flower Grows

IN THE HEART OF BELFAST, opposite the city hall, a billboard keeps the citizens current on the number of fatalities. A fortnightly newsmagazine regularly runs a calendar of violent incidents and statistical tables of injuries, burnings, kneecappings, etc. The crisis in Northern Ireland is well-chronicled and accounted for.

No one, however, as far as I know, has recorded the other side. No one has listed the names of the men and women who have found a new relationship with Jesus Christ because of the troubles. No one has compiled the spiritual victories, the conversions or the number of lives that have been changed or tried to measure the renewal taking place in the province. It's impossible, of course.

Numbers can't tell the story. A flower grows amid the rubble, and the fragrance and beauty of it set off the real ugliness of the worldly conflict around it. The following vignettes offer glimpses of that flower.

The walls of Derry are a sight to behold. For 250 years these ugly but sturdy bastions have guarded the second city of Ulster. Before they were a year old, they had withstood three major sieges. Today children reenact those sieges with homemade flags on the slopes, citizens walk their dogs along the promenade on top and tourists (very few these days) snap pictures of the ancient cannons.

Long before the present-day struggle, an idyllic valley graced the wall on the west side and a gently rising green hill rose from the valley. One day in 1848 a young Ulsterwoman paused by the wall to drink in the pastoral scene. But Mrs. Cecil Frances Alexander's thoughts were far from Ireland at that moment, and she soon penned the lines which have become a traditional Good Friday hymn:

> There is a green hill far away,
> Without a city wall,
> Where the dear Lord was crucified,
> Who died to save us all.

When Michael Barrett stood by those walls on August 12, 1969, the scene had drastically changed. The valley was now the notorious Catholic ghetto, the Bogside, and the hill a slightly more middle-class Catholic housing estate, the Creggan. Barrett had grown up in the ghetto. Like 20% of the young men in the Bogside, he was unemployed and out of school. That last week, however, he had had plenty to keep him busy. The newly formed Derry Citizens Defense Association, in preparation for the annual August 12 Protestant parade around the walls, recruited Michael and his chums. They gathered milk bottles, paving stones, clubs, marbles. At strategic points they piled material from which they could quickly build barricades, and they prepared the milk bottles for petrol (gasoline) bombs.

That morning an eerie stillness settled over the slum. While some 15,000 Protestant men and boys in dark suits, sashes and bowler hats gathered in the city for the march, the Bogside remained silent and grimly watchful. A few children played in the streets. The stewards of the Derry Citizens Defense Association began to gather in a nearby hall as the police took up positions around the edge of the area. The role of the police traditionally had been to form a physical barrier between the opposing groups. Even though the marchers flung pennies and taunts from the walls, and the Catholics generally jeered back and threw fruit and rocks, only on occasion had the annual ritual led to actual bloodshed.

This year, however, the Bogsiders were angry and afraid. In January, the RUC had invaded the area, destroyed property and beaten bystanders as they searched for provocateurs. During riots in April, the police had chased some teenagers through the home of a resident, and the man, Samuel Devenney, and several of his children were beaten. Devenney later died. Michael knew Catherine Devenney, one of the daughters who was beaten.

Trouble broke out about 2:30 p.m. In minutes Michael and others raised the barricades, and the police, egged on by the Protestant crowds, charged the area. Then the Bogside boys ran to the top of a nearby highrise where they had stockpiled petrol bombs and hurled them from the heights to repel the invading police. Not until several days later, when British troops entered the fray, did peace come to the Bogside. Then it was a shaky peace, maintained only by the presence of the army.

In the ensuing months Michael made a dozen trips back and forth from Derry to Dublin. He often drove a van belonging to a local businessman, and when he returned to Derry, a layer of rifles, pistols and ammunition lay on the floor of the van, covered with boxes and bags of dry goods. One time he stayed in the Republic for several months.

In August, 1971, however, Michael was back in Derry, unfortunately. His name by this time was on the police dossiers and the Stormont government had finally succeeded in getting London's okay to proceed with internment without trial. The IRA had warned Michael the night before, but as he left his home shortly before dawn that morning, the military police stopped him and arrested him at gun point.

They herded him, with several hundred more, behind the barbed wire at Long Kesh, a prison camp four miles outside Belfast. Twenty-four months later, without trial or without explanation, he was released.

Long Kesh changed Michael Barrett. Month after month of poor food, not enough warm clothing, and hours spent leaning

111

spread-eagle against a wall had broken his spirit. He wanted to break from the past, so when he left jail, he moved to the Falls Rd. area of Belfast at the invitation of a friend. Not that things were any better there. The Very Rev. Canon Padraig Murphy, pastor to 20,000 Roman Catholics in West Belfast, had said, "One out of ten provos (IRA) might be a republican by conviction. Three or four are gangsters, in it for money and name. The other five are young fellows not long out of school who are unemployed . . . If they could find jobs and homes they would be decent, hard-working people."

(Murphy is the same priest to whom the army appealed for help to quell a riot. Murphy walked up to a group of angry women and said, "Sure, and do you know what they tell me? That all the good-looking women are going home!" That brought a good laugh and the crowd broke and went home.)

Liam Doyle, Michael's friend, had found work as a baker's helper, and he was learning the trade. It was a small shop, and the owner was looking for another helper, so Liam talked him into hiring Michael. It was night work, hot and hard, but it was work.

The two men slept in one of the two upstairs rooms in Liam's parents' four-room house, several blocks from the Royal Victoria Hospital. The house, identical to hundreds of others built about the turn of the century, had running water but no indoor toilet. Another son slept in the living room.

In the Doyle household, before Liam and Michael left for work each evening, four or five friends would often gather in the 11' x 8' living room for tea. In Derry, however, when a group had gathered at Michael's house, the talk centered on politics. At Liam's house the conversation invariably went back to — of all things — God. Michael had spent many hours in the past talking about the church, about the priests and about religion, but these conversations in Belfast weren't like those. Some of the fellows had Bibles and they read from them. Occasionally a priest joined them, and they talked about God and about life, and sometimes they prayed.

"I couldn't take it, at first," Michael said later. "I thought

Liam had gone bananas. Then I began to listen out of curiosity. When I realized one day that I actually looked forward to tea time, well, that's when I said to myself, 'Michael Barret, you've come a long way.' "

Michael still had a ways to go, however. One evening early in 1974 two of the friends at tea reported on a meeting they had attended at the Clonard Monastery. The Clonard sits several hundred yards from the peace line, a barbed wire barricade that separates the Protestant Shankill and the Catholic Falls Rd. areas. The barrier neatly cuts in half dozens of narrow streets of row houses and British troops guard the gates. You can pass through if you wish, but few do.

That's what amazed the friends. Protestants, they reported, attended the meeting in the Clonard. A priest, several nuns, perhaps two dozen Catholics and a half-dozen Protestants sang, read the Bible, and talked about their faith and put their arms around each other while they prayed.

The Clonard meeting had been started early in 1973 by a Father McCarthy, recently returned from the U.S. McCarthy had worked in the Redemptorist Monastery many years before and returned to minister to the people in that riot-wracked area.

Protestants, who are seen frequently slipping through the lines, run great risks. One woman told a reporter, "Ordinarily, I'm the biggest coward on two feet. I have come here to go to the international prayer meetings in the darkest, most terrible times of trouble, and through that peace line. When I come I'm walking on the street, but my thoughts and my heart are up in the sky and I feel no fear." As she walked she passed patrols with blackened faces and automatic rifles.

A Presbyterian deaconess who attended the meetings told a friend, "The church officers told me either you stop going over to that papist church or else." She continued to go, but not as often.

Partly in curiosity and partly from the urging of their friends, Michael and Liam attended one of the Clonard prayer meetings. The simple choruses they sang — "His banner over me is love . . . We are one in the Spirit" — had a quality that

113

transcended the old divisions and bound the group together.

No one argued religion or theology, but different ones explained how a certain passage of Scripture meant something to them. Some told about their problems — sickness, a drunken husband, anxiety for the children — and requested prayer.

"I couldn't believe I could hold the hand of a Protestant," Michael said, "and not want to crush it. It didn't make sense. Twenty-two years of hating and now I actually felt love for these people."

At that point Michael couldn't explain in so many words what had happened to him during those months of tea-time fellowship. Today he can. "I became a real Christian. I began to believe things the priests had told me for years. I finally said 'yes' to the baptism I had received as a child and now I'm a different person."

The IRA, however, didn't understand. Because Michael worked at night, they wanted him to attend meetings and work for them in the daytime. He refused. One evening a visitor came to tea at the Doyles' and dominated the conversation. He told stories of Catholics who had had kneecaps shot off, front teeth broken, testicles burned — traditional IRA punishment for collaborators. Michael and Liam knew it was a warning and shortly after that Michael left the country.

*   *   *

Many heap blame on the churches and scorn the clergy. *Fortnightly,* a Belfast newsmagazine, wrote, ". . . the churches are not prepared to admit the full extent of their guilt. . . . They have elected to stay in their self-appointed institutional holy places, emerging only now and then to make statements of condemnation."

Conor Cruise O'Brien, respected statesman and historian from the Republic, criticized the churches for "encouraging, exalting and extending the kind of trivial-sectarian self-righteousness which forms a culture in which violence so easily multiplies."

Individual stories, however, belie the accusations. One minister sat in his office just minutes before a Sunday evening service when word came of trouble down the street. "My place is down there," he said, and ran from the church. At the riot scene he found two groups hurling rocks and bottles and curses. He also found an Anglican rector, two curates, a parish priest and a Methodist minister. The clergymen linked arms and formed a human barrier between the two mobs.

*　　*　　*

Scores of fine points and petty distinctions separate religious groups in Ulster. Not only do Catholics and Protestants eye each other across the gulf, but the various Protestant denominations, as a rule, find it hard to cooperate.

The spirit permeates the young. One church bulletin tells of two small boys who responded to the Gospel message at a children's meeting.

"I got Jesus in my heart under the bridge," one told the other. "Did you get him there?"

"No," replied the other. "But I got him in my heart before I went to bed."

"Oh, no, you didn't," the first one shot back. "It must be under the bridge."

*　　*　　*

Downtown Belfast will shock a visitor. The IRA campaign to paralyze commerce blew the heart out of the inner city. Rubble now replaces office buildings. Holes remain where department stores once stood. Troops monitor traffic with massive iron grilles and chains. In one nine-month period, 130 bombs exploded within 300 yards of a church house.

Sixteen bombs have blasted the Parish Church of St. George. The windows are boarded, and with the furnace turned up full, the sanctuary doesn't get much above 45 degrees.

The rector, however, is optimistic. He told a *Reader's Digest* editor, "After a really bad blast, one feels depressed. But the way our people have cleared the rubbish has been encouraging. Throughout all the troubles, not a single person has left the choir. They keep coming, twice every Sunday. That makes me realize how important it is to keep the witness of a parish like this going."

*　　*　　*

Andersontown in West Belfast is a solid Catholic enclave. When Women Together, a peace movement spearheaded by a Catholic woman, staged a demonstration, a much smaller group of militant women broke it up. The IRA Provisionals there claimed responsibility for the tarring and feathering of a pregnant mother of five. Afterwards she was beaten with hurling (Irish hockey) sticks and tied to a lamp post.

A young man in Andersonstown, call him Joseph, became a Christian. His father had been a leader in the civil rights movement which provoked the current round of troubles.

Joseph found opportunities for Christian work in the army camps, but, because of who he was, had to carry it on in secret. He thought no one knew. One day as he rode the bus to work, someone leaned over him and said, "We know what you're doing. You'd better get out of this country, quick." Shortly after that he left.

*　　*　　*

More than one flower in the rubble of Northern Ireland has been trampled on by callousness. The Rev. Joseph Parker, senior chaplain of the Mission to Seamen, lost his only child, a fourteen-year-old boy, when a bomb exploded in a car. Parker began to crusade for nonviolence and peace. He urged that a chapel on the Antrim Road, about to be demolished, be set aside as a meeting place where Irishmen could come together and learn to trust each other. The parish that owned the building turned him down.

116

He began a work he called "Witness for Peace," and blanketed Belfast with signs, but he received very little support for his pains. Instead, he told the local newspaper, his colleagues deserted him. "I am a very sad man, a very lonely man . . . I am extremely disappointed about how things have gone with me."

Parker finally gave up and moved with his wife to Canada.

* * *

Several years before the troubles flared up again, the Rev. Ray Davey felt the need for a center for reconciliation and began Corrymeela. That's Gaelic for "Hill of Harmony."

He found a resort center on the cliffs overlooking the ocean some fifty miles north of Belfast and began inviting Catholics and Protestants to come. In one year recently, some 6000 did — to rest, worship together and learn to live in peace.

Davey tells the story of two groups of school boys, Catholic and Protestant, from the ghettos. The first day they kept to their respected groups and eyed each other. At night they barricaded their doors. The next day when each group learned what the other had done, it broke the ice. Those two groups have returned to Corrymeela many times and now occasionally cross the neighborhood barriers to visit each other.

Corrymeela brings small groups in the city together. Vans carry the young people from their communities to a neutral hall, then bring them back. Many young people have developed lasting friendships with those on the other side, but Davey refuses to speak of success. "You peg away at the problem," he says, "not because you expect any success. We may never make any significant contribution, but we'll try because we believe in it."

* * *

Jimmy Murphy, the same indefatigable Brethren businessman we talked about before, regularly tapes broadcasts for his friends in America. Most of them are vignettes of spiritual victories. One such broadcast ran:

This is Jimmy Murphy in Belfast. I am often asked about the long-term effects of the troubles on Christians in Ulster. Of course, it's early to be drawing conclusions, but already I can see changes.

Most noticeable are the crippling effects on the lives of those who have been severely injured — the white stick of blindness, the artificial limb, the wheelchair, the crutch which can't be hidden. Equally, the white scars and pock marks left by lacerations and the blotches of plastic surgery are impossible to hide with powder and cream on a young girl's face. These (and there are many) will limp through life and endure the embarrassment that comes with not being normal.

What effect has this had on their spiritual life? Of course, I cannot speak for all, but I know a godly man who lost both his legs in a bomb blast and is now confined to a wheelchair. A friend saw him recently sitting in the sunshine at the Park gate, his face beaming as he witnessed for His Lord to all who passed by. Not a word of recrimination; just full of love to God. There is a saying — "Where there's life, there's hope." In Ulster we've rewritten that saying to, "Where there's life, there's love!"

For the past few weeks in our studios each Wednesday night, a team has been working on a new three-part Christmas drama. That's usual at this time of year, but what is not usual is that this play was written by a young school teacher who was caught in a double bomb blast. She was blown through a first-floor window into the street below, lost one leg, and received terrible lacerations to her face and body. As she recovered she found a new door of Christian witness open to her — she is a writer. We're all excited about her first radio drama. We have been praying for months that God would raise up Christian writers to supply the scripts for this vital work that is being heard on radio stations around the world.

I know another young Christian who, at a conference on

personal evangelism, confessed he was not living as he knew God would have him live. A few months later a large bomb virtually wrecked the entire stone building in which he worked. Others were rushed to a hospital, but not until hours later did a friend find him lying in a back yard unconscious, severely cut and almost dead from loss of blood. For days the doctors feared for his life, but when I spoke to him on the phone recently he was very much alive and on fire for God. When you've been close to death, the things of this world don't matter too much anymore. He was excited about a wonderful work just a few miles from where he lives. More than 100 had given their lives to Jesus Christ and a new church was established.

There are many more — for example, a kitchen supervisor who was actually looking into a car when it exploded. Her injuries were beyond description: broken legs and arms, lacerations all over her body, face burned almost beyond recognition. Her life hung in the balance for days, yet today her shining Christian witness is a benediction to everyone in the hospital.

Then there is the case of a Christian shop owner who was warned by a boy of 14 that the car parked outside had a bomb in it. As they ran out, the bomb exploded and killed the boy. She was severely injured and has had to have extensive skin grafts to her legs. She was taken to a Roman Catholic hospital where she received excellent attention, and as she recovered she witnessed daily to the saving power of God.

I could go on, but these incidents clearly show how the troubles have led to a deeper spiritual life for many.

* * *

Another Jimmy Murphy broadcast ran:

Only that doctrine which stands the test in the face of death is worth having. I remember an old friend of my parents visiting our home about twenty years ago. He was a small, square man who spoke with a strong German accent, and at that time had just returned from working amongst displaced persons in

Western Germany. With deep earnestness he told how the Communists had subdued the Iron Curtain countries. He spoke of informers' constant surveillance, and ceaseless questioning. Almost everyone dismissed him as a fanatic. They said he had become unbalanced in his judgment from living too close to the problem. These things could never happen here, certainly not in Ulster.

I thought of him recently as I listened to a man tell of an experience he never wants to endure again. While on private business in one of the terrorist-occupied areas of Belfast, a gunman confronted him and forced him to drive to a house deep in a Catholic area. Inside his captors searched him and kept him under constant watch. An hour later an intelligence officer arrived. He took this man's diary and personal papers and spread them on the table before him, then began a thorough examination of his private life that lasted almost two hours. Later they released him with threats to his wife and family if he revealed anything about his captors.

Instantly I was back 20 years, and I could hear the old man's voice as he told about people who were lifted for no apparent reason and taken away for questioning for hours, then released after being warned what would happen if they talked. "How did you feel?" I asked. He said, "I was terrified. I expected to be shot at any minute. I could see myself ending up in some river."

I knew this man was a Christian, so I asked him "Did you pray?"

"Jimmy," he said, "I remember going up the stairs into that little room. I remember the children playing on the street and a woman going about her work. I remember thinking, well, this is it. And in those moments I said, 'God I'm Yours. There's no one else who can help me now,' and I committed everything into His hands."

That kind of commitment has a certainty which cannot be described, only experienced. It is the very heartbeat of the new life in Christ Jesus.

Is It a Religious War?

CHAPTER ELEVEN

Is It a Religious War?

Interviewer: What do you have against Roman Catholics?
Belfast Protestant: Are you daft? Why, their religion,
of course.   — *BBC-TV* 1970

THE CROWDS ALONG CASTLE PLACE in the center of Belfast
wear no badges of loyalty to one community or the other. No
sectarian stamp indicates Protestant or Catholic. You rub
shoulders with shoppers in Marks and Spencer or in Woolworths
and you can't tell which side they're from. The couple at the
counter in the Copper Griddle may be Republican or Loyalist.
They pay the same prices, drink the same tea and walk outside
to breathe the same soot-filled air.

Yet this mix of humanity is rare in Northern Ireland. In
very few places do the two communities integrate unnoticed.
Scratch the surface of society and you find two groups, each
with its own cultural and religious heritage which has led to
distinct patterns of life.

The maps you buy of Belfast and Londonderry which divide
the city into various shaded areas of Protestant, Catholic or
mixed show how the size of the mixed areas has decreased
dramatically since 1968. Find out a man's name and address
and you generally know his religion. Often you can tell by just
knowing where he works. The name of the school he went to
is almost proof positive of which side he is on, and the newspaper

he reads, the TV channel he watches and the bus he takes home offer further evidence of both his religious and political leanings.

More than 1,200 persons have been killed and millions of dollars worth of property destroyed since the violence started up again in '68. Barbed wire and armed patrols divide certain sections of Belfast and Protestant and Catholic paramilitary groups bomb and snipe and cow the general public.

What is at the heart of the conflict? Is it race, nationality, religion? Is it, as the casual observer easily concludes, a religious war between Protestants and Catholics?

The ugly spectacle of two Christian bodies resolving their differences through violence makes most Christians shudder. Yet bloody battles in the name of Christianity are nothing new. Immediately following the Reformation, Catholic-Protestant wars raged over Europe. Persecution, assassinations and massacres in which princes, priests and reformers played major roles dominated the history of the continent for a century.

The Ulster struggle, at first glance, appears to be an anachronistic throwback to the sixteenth century, a historical hangover to give the church a headache and remind it of the sins of the past. A deeper look reveals it to be much more than that.

There is a case for throwing the cause and the blame for the deep sectarian feelings back to England. Without question, over the years the Westminster government inflamed the animosities between the two groups as a means of controlling the country. For example, when Irish lands were confiscated, the justification offered was protection against the papacy. Actually, it was protection against Spain and France which England had in mind.

The Bill of Rights of 1689 and the Penal Laws of the early 1700's deprived Catholics of civil rights such as education, owning property and participation in public life. Lord Randolph Churchill, trying to oust the liberal Gladstone as prime minister in 1886 played what he called "the Orange Card." He kindled the fears of Northern Protestants to believe that "home rule would mean Roman rule."

H. M. Carson, a minister in Bangor, points a finger at history but aims it at the sixteenth century reformers. He says they failed to deal with the Roman view of the state as sacred, and cites men such as John Calvin and John Knox who thought in terms of national churches. When the seventeenth century planters came to Ulster, they came not only as English and Scots but as Anglicans and Presbyterians. The cause of Ulster soon became the cause of Christ, and the conflict one between the people of God and the people not of God. Carson adds, parenthetically, that when you see what the so-called Protestant population is like, you realize how absurd that idea is.

"Under this kind of thinking," Carson wrote, "the Protestant minister becomes an Elijah on Mt. Carmel facing the apostate ruler . . . and confronting the priests of Baal (for Baal read the Roman Catholic church).

"By New Testament standards, however, this is a false equation. No one nation today stands where Old Testament Israel stood. The Church of Christ is not the religious aspect of the nation but is the community of faith drawn out of the nation."

Carson is one of many who bemoan the political involvement of ministers, especially as they commit the church to a political position. While he doesn't name the Rev. Ian Paisley in his writings, Carson is aware that Paisley is the chief exponent of this position.

It is difficult to deny that it is a religious struggle when a man clearly states that he is fighting a religious battle. For him, no doubt, it is religious. The following passage, for example, from Paisley's *Protestant Telegraph* is typical of his arguments:

"Ulster Protestants are passing through a time of tremendous testing. The Socialist government at Westminster is intent on their destruction. Harold Wilson, the puppet of Cardinal Heenan, and Mr. Callaghan, the puppet of Harold Wilson, are out for our destruction. Ulster is, in fact, to all intents and purposes under direct Westminster control, with a military dictatorship geared to placate the Roman Catholics and browbeat and 'jackboot' the Protestants." (The Protestant siege mentality comes through here as strongly as the anti-Catholicism.)

In other articles or speeches Paisley clearly states that it is

125

a religious battle and the enemy is the Church of Rome. Much of the *Protestant Telegraph* is devoted to anti-Catholic articles such as "Betrayal of the Faith" or "Unity with the Church of Rome — Never!"

Paisley's anti-Catholic rhetoric has contributed immeasurably to the hardening of sectarian positions in the last six or seven years. How, for example, does someone on either side respond when he reads in the *Protestant Telegraph* an article about the sale of Hitler statuettes in Germany. The manufacturers were considering Mussolini statuettes for Italy and the *Protestant Telegraph* suggested that they "make a statuette of the greatest war criminal that was never hanged, Pope Pius XII."

Paisley's speeches, however, are filled with more than bigotry and hatred. They are violent in nature and have contributed directly, as the Cameron Commission concluded, to riots and to bloodshed.

Just how influential is Ian Paisley and his *Protestant Telegraph?* No doubt he stepped into a leadership vacuum in the early seventies and struck a responsive chord with a majority of the Protestant working class. Then, as positions hardened, he swung many moderates behind him. And, as Albert Menendez says in *The Bitter Harvest,* "It is doubtful that ultimate peace can come to Ulster unless the Protestants who subscribe to these views can be convinced that their fears are largely groundless."

While for Paisley it is a religious battle fought on the political level, many of his followers no doubt are more interested in the political part of it. Close associates of Paisley formed the Ulster Protestant Volunteers and some of these were no doubt instrumental in reorganizing the Ulster Volunteer Force. The original UVF was the illegal Protestant paramilitary group formed by Lord Edward Carson in 1912, and it forced the division of Northern and Southern Ireland. Since it was reorganized in the late sixties, the UVF has been responsible for dozens of bombings, shootings and deaths. Most outside observers agree that the Rev. Ian Paisley's rhetoric gave birth to the new Protestant volunteer movement.

A second focal point for anti-Catholicism in Northern Ireland is the Orange Order. At the close of the eighteenth century, Protestants, again feeling the threat of the Catholic majority, began forming secret societies which coalesced into the Orange Order. Its main purpose has always been to maintain Protestant supremacy, and it is impossible today to measure the immense influence which it has on the social and political life of the country.

For example, the Orange Order controlled the Unionist Party which controlled Northern Ireland for 50 years. Few Unionist politicians held office without the approval of the Orange Order. Yet its leaders say it is basically religious and only coincidentally political.

The Orange Order is a major factor in keeping Protestants convinced that the real enemy is Rome, and many rank and file Orangemen (some 100,000 in Ulster) believe that the Vatican was behind the civil rights protests as a ploy in its plan for world conquest.

On July 12 each year the Orange Order sponsors the marches which, on dozens of occasions, have led to violence. Thousands of orange-sashed marchers with bowler hats, beating large drums, parade through the streets.

Their very presence provokes strong Catholic antagonism and they often feed these feelings with anti-Catholic taunts and jeers. These, in turn, bring stones, rocks and bottles down on the marchers and the battle is on.

This, by the way, is the organization that teaches its members to respond, when asked why they are Orangemen, "Because I desire to live to the Glory of God, and, resisting every superstition and idolatry, earnestly to contend for the faith once delivered to the saints." And a favorite piece of Orange poetry runs:

> "Here's to the lily that dear Orange flower.
> Here's to the bright purple heather,
> The emblem of men who defied popish power.
> Here's to the Orange and purple together.
> So fill every glass; let the toast pass.
> Down with popery, priest and the mass."

127

How much does the Protestant in the North actually have to fear from a Roman Catholic dominated government?

The question is almost irrelevant to the current struggle. It is how the Protestant perceives it that makes the difference today. The tendency is to fight the phantom created by doubt and fear rather than to respond to what is real. However, he doesn't have to dig deeply to make his case.

To begin with he can cite the constitution of the Republic of Ireland which "recognizes the special position of the Holy Catholic Apostolic and Roman Church as the guardian of the Faith professed by a great majority of the citizens."

Then he can quote Eamon de Valera, the patriot, statesman, and for many years, the leader of the Republic. "Since the coming of St. Patrick 1,500 years ago, Ireland has been a Christian and a Catholic nation. All the ruthless attempts made down through the centuries to force us from this allegiance have not shaken her faith. She remains a Catholic nation."

He can also go back not too many years and find isolated instances of persecution, of blatant bias of civic officials and judges. Then he can point to areas of legislation — divorce, abortion, sale of contraceptives — in which the church has certainly made its will felt. As Conor Cruise O'Brien put it, democracy in Ireland has to be taken with a tincture of theocracy.

In recent years the church hierarchy has backed off somewhat in its insistence on a Catholic state. The primate of all Ireland, Cardinal Conway, said he would have no objections to the repeal of Article 44-1.2 (which proclaims Ireland a Catholic state), and the church also rescinded a ban on Catholics attending Protestant Trinity College.

Northern Protestants, however, are not without genuine cause for concern when they think of a United Ireland. "The state of the (95 percent) Catholic nation can fairly be criticized for a certain insensitivity in relation to the rights and claims of the 5 percent minority," Conor Cruise O'Brien wrote.

Certainly many Catholic Republicans in the North see the conflict in terms of nationalism rather than religion. George

Bernard Shaw wrote, ". . . if you break a nation's nationality it will think of nothing else but getting it set again. It will listen to no reformer, no philosopher and no preacher, until the demands of the nationalist are granted. It will attend to no business, however vital, except the business of unification and liberation."

But the common man as well as the leadership in the Republic of Ireland has pretty much disproved this. While they often pay respect to the cause of the Northern Catholic, they don't offer much more today than sympathy. They have their own problems. A united Ireland is way down the priority list, and, besides, it would bring in all kinds of economic problems without the subsidies of Great Britain — which is nearly bankrupt itself.

So, with the exception of a minority handful of idealists or drifters or misfits, the Irish in the South leave the North to fight its own problems. (There is enough sympathy to give refuge to the IRA — as long as they don't rock the boat in the South.)

For the Catholic in the North, however, it is a different story. For 50 years he has been a politically disenfranchised second-class citizen. Many Protestants will admit to discrimination of Catholics, although they often rationalize it as "their own fault." Independent study groups have documented many cases, even though the Government of Ireland Act of 1920 expressly forbids religious discrimination.

Naturally, the minority Catholic in the North looks to the Republic for his salvation. And while he may have a smug attitude about his own church being the "one true church," he is definitely more interested in gaining his civil rights than in propagating his faith as the only religion. To him, the Protestant descendants of the British and Scottish planters are still colonialists. It is still a conflict between the oppressed and the oppressor and a united Ireland is the answer.

(Often through the last 50 years the Catholic in the North has seen the IRA as the means to reach his goal. The riots of '68, and especially the occupation of the British army, provided the impetus to rebuild the illegal guerilla group.)

129

Religiously segregated education does as much to shape a child's political biases as his religious ones. Parish priests give little respect to the regime and Catholic schools generally refuse to fly the Union Jack or sing the national anthem.

Bernadette Devlin wrote, "I went to a militantly Republican grammar school and, under its influence, began to revolt against the Establishment, on the simple rule of thumb, highly satisfying to a ten-year-old, that Irish equals good, English equals bad."

There is still another group, the young socialists and Marxists who gave impetus to the civil rights marches, who see the conflict in terms of a class struggle. Both the Stormont and Dublin governments are bourgeois governments to be overthrown. The churches have not taken the part of the people, but have sided with the Establishment and should be closed and locked. Bernadette Devlin, one of those young socialists, wrote, "Among the best traitors Ireland has ever had, Mother Church ranks at the very top, a massive obstacle in the path of equality and freedom." Many of the IRA leaders have been and are today politically to the left. James Connolly, the Irish activist who led the 1916 uprising, was a Marxist and the "official" branch of the IRA is strongly socialist.

One thing the Northern Ireland conflict is not is a theological quarrel. No one is fighting for a particular creed or a doctrine. No minute points of theology, modes of baptism or interpretations of particular passages of Scripture dominate the rhetoric of either side.

Nor is persecution a real factor. Catholics worship as they will. So do Protestants, even in the Republic.

To what extent, then, are the churches to blame for the current situation? "Have they," Bernadette Devlin asks, "all forgotten the . . . fundamentals of Christianity, 'Love your enemy'? No," she answers. "They rationalize it by saying the people they disapprove of are the enemies of God and so they justify their hatred of people who never did them any harm."

But could they, if they so desired, exert more influence for peace? Certainly they have made the expected pronouncements.

At regular intervals, or after some particularly bloody incident, leading churchmen deplore the violence and the current state of war. Bishop so and so "condemns the foul and callous murder of the widow Murphy," or, "The moderator of the such and such church said "When will we come to our senses and sit down together to work out our differences?" Every major church group has made a dozen such statements, and hundreds of sermons on peace, brotherhood, non-violence, etc. have been preached. The Catholic Bishop of Ardagh and Clonmacnois, Cahal B. Daly, published an entire book of his writings and speeches entitled, *Violence in Ireland and the Christian Conscience.*

But all too often the speeches of churchmen, while calling for an end to violence, also heap fuel on fire by pinning blame on the other side. After the bitter battles of Belfast and Londonderry in August, 1969, Cardinal Conway called on his people to "remember that Protestants in general are good Christian people." Yet, at the same time, he threw the blame at the feet of Protestant mobs. Immediately three leading Protestants attacked the cardinal's statement (which came closer to the conclusions of most outside observers).

Protestant and Catholic clergy, of course, have been conditioned by the same culture and history as their flocks. They also feel the weight of heavy community pressure. Any sign of reconciliation or offer of peace may be taken as weakness or straying from the faith and could bring on them the scorn of their own people.

In spite of this, some Christian leaders have risen above sectarianism. Shortly before Christmas eight Protestant churchmen met with IRA leaders to help bring about a temporary cease-fire. Others such as Protestants Sydney Callaghan and Cecil Kerr and Catholics Desmond Wilson and Padraig Murphy have braved scorn and recriminations to make meaningful contact with the other side. But they are a minority.

Christians, of course, find it hard to admit that that which is so central in their lives — their faith — can be a factor in a shameful scandal such as that in Northern Ireland. No doubt faith is not to blame. But that which has passed for religion in Ireland and in many parts of the world since the fall of man has certainly been, and remains today, a large part of the problem. On top of that, the churches and church leaders who bear the name of Christ have contributed significantly to the blot on His name.

The Future

CHAPTER TWELVE

The Future

WHAT ABOUT THE FUTURE of Northern Ireland? When will the violence stop? Will there be civil war? And what part will Christians and churches play?

After you have been in the country for awhile, asking questions, talking to pastors, businessmen, people on the street, you get a vague feeling of something missing. People are very willing to talk about the troubles. In fact when you steer the conversation away from it, they come right back. But you soon realize that they're talking only about the past or the present. No one alludes to the future, except with a wistful, "Where will it all end?" But there are no prophets in Northern Ireland. Ask the man on the street what he thinks is going to happen tomorrow, and he will most likely shrug off the question.

It is popular now for writers and commentators to project scenarios. If this happened then something else would happen, a cause and effect relationship. Usually they devise a benign and a malign scenario, an optimistic and a pessimistic course of events. But they still avoid pointing to one or the other as the most probable.

Cecil Kerr, for example, says, "I see two pictures in my mind, one a very frightening one. I know some of the ideologists behind what's happening, and their great desire (and some are prepared to die for it) is to see an all-out socialist republic in which God will be dead and the churches will be locked and barred, archaic monuments of the past.

"The other picture is one of Ireland united, not politically, but united in Christ and in the power of the Spirit." Then he adds, "It can go either way."

Still, Kerr is optimistic. He points out that before the Vatican Council, Roman Catholics were dissuaded from buying the Bible. Today they are buying them by the hundreds. This is the greatest day of opportunity for sharing the Word of God that Ireland has ever known — ever, in all its history.

Kerr's scenarios are extremes, but not any more so than those of Conor Cruise O'Brien's. O'Brien is perhaps the most respected voice inside Ireland by Ireland watchers on the outside and follows no traditional party line. In his book, *States of Ireland,* he sketches a benign model in which the IRA offensive will collapse. The political prisoners jailed without trial will be released. The two sides will begin discussions out of which will emerge new structures. Local communities will receive more autonomy. More and more the two sides will find they can live with these changes.

In his malignant model O'Brien sees the Catholic offensive and the Protestant counter-offensive escalating. The IRA will grow stronger. The British army will finally pull out and all-out civil war in the North will begin. Thousands of Catholics will flee to the south and the west. Protestants will flee to the north and the east. Finally Ireland would be left with two states again, each one more homogeneous than in the past and each one led by a right wing government. Possibly the United Nations would finally agree to patrol the border.

None of these scenarios is realistic, except, possibly, O'Brien's second scene. Why, after more than 300 years of division and hate and fighting should the two sides suddenly move toward peaceful relations and a final answer to the problem? It is more likely that during our lifetime, barring the influence of extreme changes in the world outside of Ireland, the situation will muddle along much as it has in the past 50 years with off and on periods of peace.

At the moment, after six years of the troubles, the IRA has shown a few signs of willingness to negotiate. There is a war weariness on both sides which makes it harder to maintain the community support which paramilitary groups need to exist.

The Loyalists show less signs of backing off, but, traditionally, when they can no longer imagine a threat to their way of life and security, they will lay down their clubs and paving stones. The siege mentality won't disappear, but it will rest lightly in the hearts of thousands of Protestant Ulstermen.

Outside of Ireland we live with a myth that the killing in Northern Ireland is primarily the work of the Irish Republican Army. The truth is that since 1972, when the killing increased dramatically, Loyalist (Protestant) paramilitary groups have been responsible for more sectarian killings than the other side.

For the first few years it was the IRA pitted against the British army. Groups such as the Ulster Volunteer Force and the Ulster Defense Association were active, but adopted a more defensive posture. But by 1972 the political situation had spawned a Protestant backlash. According to two *Belfast Telegraph* reporters, "There can be no questioning the simple truth that the greater part of the near-200 such assassinations were committed by Protestants organized in groups, often for this specific purpose." Many of the killings, so often assumed by the outsider to be the work of the IRA, were the work of frustrated men who assumed the system was about to be destroyed.

"The anger, the bitterness of the people who felt their only crime had been loyalty, was translated into the most ruthless and dedicated campaign of civilian killings that had been seen in Western Europe since the Second World War."

It is easy to infer from American news reports that if the IRA would simply call a truce and cease all operations, the country would return to normal. At what point the Loyalist groups would back down, however, is another question.

Everyone in Northern Ireland knows the statistics related to the troubles. How many were killed last month or bombed this week is coffee conversation in every shop and office in the country. With the IRA truces around Christmas 1974 and early in 1975, the statistics dropped. Whether that reflected a genuine change in the strategy of the extremists or a temporary lull is hard to tell.

Many Christians are praying for revival and for peace, but the two are inseparably linked in their minds. There seems to be an assumption that if God is going to do anything it must be to bring an end to the troubles. Peace is viewed more politically than spiritually. The most frequently quoted Scripture verse in the country may be II Chronicles 7: 14.

For many the direct response of God to prayer and repentance just has to be a return to life the way it was before the troubles began. H. M. Carson in Bangor seems to be saying this when he writes, "Ulster's greatest need is an extraordinary visitation by God. We have had political and military solutions for centuries." And because of the attention on Ulster as a world news item, he claims that "revival in Ulster could have world-wide repercussions." Clearly, he is one of those who assumes that revival, if it comes, will affect the political life of the country.

Of course there is a case for that. If Christ genuinely changes a life, it will show up in behavior. If love and patience and long-suffering and peace replace hatred and bigotry and fear and unrest in lives on a large scale, why shouldn't we expect it to touch all areas of life?

This assumes that either revival will reach the leaders of established churches and political organizations or that the rank and file exercise enough influence on the leadership to bring about change. In Ulster you can't assume either.

Cecil Kerr's optimistic scenario may be closer to the truth than anything else. He ignores the political realm and postulates a united Ireland on a spiritual level. Again, that may sound idealistic but at least he recognizes that the peace which is a result of the prayers of many Christian people has nothing to do with negotiations of governments or groups.

There are encouraging signs in Northern Ireland, some of which we've mentioned in these pages. Many people pray for Ireland, and God will still use the man or woman who is completely committed to him. There is the Protestant pastor who takes his people caroling in a Catholic section, the mill worker who lost both his legs but doesn't have a bitter bone in his body, the Catholic businessman who leads a mixed prayer meeting, the young man who once threw rocks at the soldiers but now plays gospel songs on his guitar in the army canteen.

The skeptic points to Ireland today as a glaring example of the divisiveness and the destructiveness of religion. And to the world, this land which once bore saints and scholars reveals a dearth of both. History, however, will record the answer to the prayer which is heard more and more in Northern Ireland these days:

> Lord, make us instruments of thy peace.
> Where there is hatred, let us sow love;
> Where there is injury, pardon;
> Where there is discord, union;
> Where there is doubt, faith;
> Where there is despair, hope;
> Where there is darkness, light;
> Where there is sadness, joy;
> Grant that we may not seek so much to be
> consoled as to console;
> to be understood, as to understand;
> to be loved, as to love;
> For it is in giving we receive, in
> pardoning we are pardoned, and in dying
> we are born into eternal life.
>   St. Francis of Assisi

139

GLOSSARY

Alliance Party — a non-sectarian political party formed in 1971. Has had only very small representation.

Black and Tans — paramilitary group of ex-servicemen which the British brought into Ireland around 1919 to help suppress the republican movement. Black and Tans referred to the uniforms which were hastily pulled together from police tunics and army pants.

Devlin, Bernadette — leader of student socialist movement in late sixties which helped instigate the civil rights movement. She was a leader in the loosely formed political group, the People's Democracy, and became a Member of Parliament at Westminster. In 1973 she married Michael McAliskey.

Internment — jailing of suspected extremists on suspicion. On August 9, 1971, the British army, under the Special Powers Act, arrested 342 IRA suspects. While many of these were subsequently released, the policy of jailing without benefit of trial or other civil rights has continued.

IRA — Irish Republican Army — an illegal paramilitary organization which has fought for some 50 years for the complete independence of all of Ireland from Great Britain and for the unity of the North and South.

Irish Free State — name of the political entity formed by the Government of Ireland Act in 1920, comprising 26 counties (all except the six of Northern Ireland). Name later changed to Republic of Ireland.

John Bull — symbol for England (roughly equivalent to use of Uncle Sam as symbol of United States).

Loyalist — one who wants Northern Ireland to be politically part of the Republic of Ireland.

Orange Order — a religious, fraternal organization founded in 1795 to maintain Protestant ascendancy. Today it dominates Northern Ireland's social and political life and, until recently, few Protestant politicians ran for office without Orange Order endorsement.

Peoples' Democracy — leftist student group formed at Queen's University in 1968 and active in the civil rights demonstrations of 1968 and 1969.

Stormont — seat of Northern Ireland government.

Ulster — the northernmost province of Ireland, comprised of the six counties which make up Northern Ireland, plus three counties in the Republic of Ireland. The name Ulster is often used loosely referring to Northern Ireland.

Ulster Defense Association — a Protestant paramilitary organization which has, in effect, declared war on the IRA and has claimed responsibility for the killing of many Catholics. There have been a number of such organizations in the 50 year history of Northern Ireland and the UDA is a recent one.

Ulster Volunteer Force — Protestant paramilitary organization. First organized by Lord Carson some 50 years ago as a threat to gain political independence. Revived in 1966, it has declared war on the IRA and has been responsible for much of the violence in recent years.

Unionist — Protestant-oriented political party in Northern Ireland which favors union with Great Britain and which has held the power in Northern Ireland politics for some 50 years.

Westminster — seat of the British government.

FACTS ABOUT NORTHERN IRELAND

Northern Ireland is comprised of six of the nine counties of the province of Ulster: Antrim, Armagh, Down, Londonderry, Tyrone, and Fermanagh. The remaining three counties of Ulster — Donegal, Monaghan and Cavan — are part of the Republic of Ireland.

Area: 5,242 square miles (roughly equivalent to the State of Connecticut)

Capital: Belfast—population 400,000

Second city: Londonderry—population 55,000

Population: 1,500,000

Roman Catholics	497,000
Protestants	929,000
Presbyterians	413,000
Church of Ireland	345,000
Methodists	72,000

Recent emigration rate: appox. 1,000 per month

FOR FURTHER READING

The Bitter Harvest: Church and State in Northern Ireland, Albert Menendez; Robert B. Luce, Washington, D. C.

The Charismatic Renewal and the Irish Experience, Thomas Flynn; Hodder and Stoughton, London.

Fire Over Ulster, Patrick Riddell; Hamish Hamilton, London.

Governing Without Consensus: An Irish Perspective, Richard Rose; Beacon Press, Boston.

Ireland's Hope, Phillip Streeter, Logos International, Plainfield, N. J.

W. P. Nicholson: Flame for God in Ulster, S. W. Murray; private edition.

Northern Ireland — A Report on the Conflict, the London Sunday Times Insight Team; Random House, New York.

Northern Ireland: Captive of History, Gary MacEoin; Holt, Rinehard and Winston, New York.

Northern Ireland: Crisis and Conflict, John Magee; Routledge & Kegan Paul, Boston.

The Northern Ireland Problem: A Study in Group Relations, Denis P. Barritt and Charles F. Carter; Oxford University Press, London.

Political Murder in Northern Ireland, Martin Dillon and Denis Lehand; Penguin Books, London.

The Price of My Soul, Bernadette Devlin; Random House, New York.

States of Ireland, Conor Cruise O'Brien; Pantheon Books, New York.

The UVF 1966-73, David Boulton; Torc Books, Dublin.

Violence in Northern Ireland and Christian Conscience, Cahal B. Daly; Veritas Publications, Dublin.

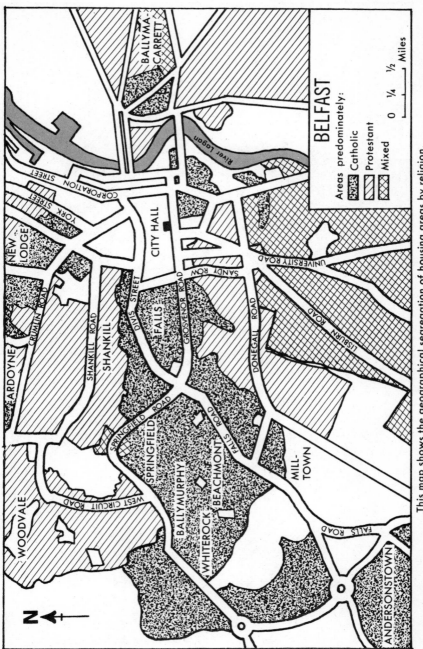

This map shows the geographical segregation of housing areas by religion.

BELFAST

Areas predominately:
- Catholic
- Protestant
- Mixed

0   ¼   ½   Miles

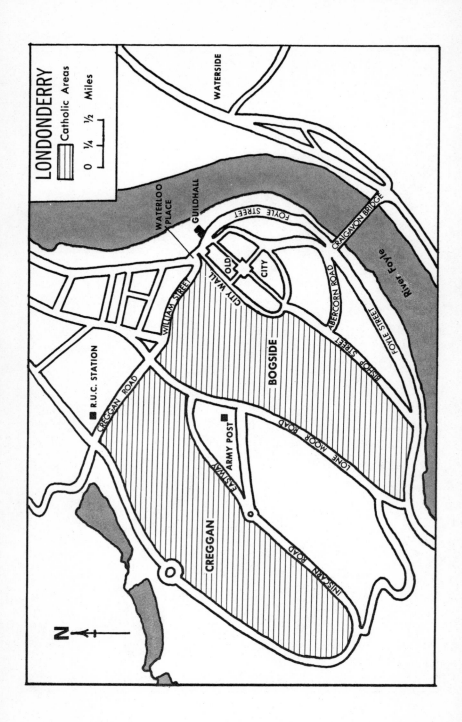

IRELAND

•••• Provincial boundaries

Areas included
in Northern Ireland

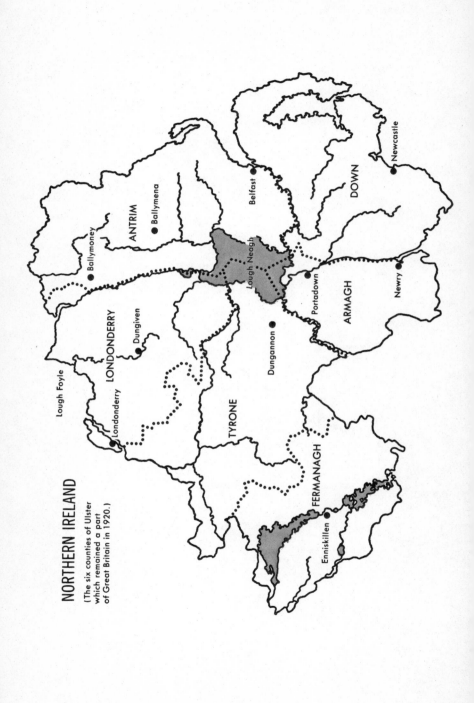

NORTHERN IRELAND

(The six counties of Ulster
which remained a part
of Great Britain in 1920.)

Lough Foyle

Londonderry

LONDONDERRY

Dungiven

Ballymoney

ANTRIM

Ballymena

Belfast

Lough Neagh

DOWN

Newcastle

Portadown

ARMAGH

Newry

Dungannon

TYRONE

FERMANAGH

Enniskillen